Cristiano Ronaldo: The Inspiring Story of One of Soccer's Star Forwards

An Unauthorized Biography

By: Clayton Geoffreys

Copyright © 2024 by Calvintir Books, LLC

All rights reserved. Neither this book nor any portion thereof may be reproduced or used in any manner whatsoever without the express written permission. Published in the United States of America.

Disclaimer: The following book is for entertainment and informational purposes only. The information presented is without contract or any type of guarantee assurance. While every caution has been taken to provide accurate and current information, it is solely the reader's responsibility to check all information contained in this article before relying upon it. Neither the author nor publisher can be held accountable for any errors or omissions. Under no circumstances will any legal responsibility or blame be held against the author or publisher for any reparation, damages, or monetary loss due to the information presented, either directly or indirectly. This book is not intended as legal or medical advice. If any such specialized advice is needed, seek a qualified individual for help.

Trademarks are used without permission. Use of the trademark is not authorized by, associated with, or sponsored by the trademark owners. All trademarks and brands used within this book are used with no intent to infringe on the trademark owners and only used for clarifying purposes.

This book is not sponsored by or affiliated with the Sporting CP B, Sporting CP, Manchester United, Real Madrid, Juventus, Al Nassr, Taça de Portugal, FA Cup, Copa del Rey, Coppa Italia, King Cup, Football League Cup, UEFA Champions League, UEFA Cup, FA Community Shield, FIFA Club World Cup, Real Sociedad, Supercopa de España, its teams, the players, or anyone involved with them.

Visit my website at www.claytongeoffreys.com
Cover photo by Student News Agency is licensed under CC BY 4.0 / modified from original

Table of Contents

Foreword 1

Introduction 3

Chapter 1: Childhood and Early Life 7

Chapter 2: Sporting CP Senior Team 13

Chapter 3: Manchester United 18

    2003-2006: Slow Start and Developmental Years 18

    2006-2007 Season: World Cup Drama and Breakout Season 21

    2007-2008 Season: Rise to Global Superstardom 23

    2008-2009: Ronaldo's Final Season at Manchester United 27

Chapter 4: Real Madrid 30

    2009-2011: Headlining Real Madrid's Second Galácticos Era 30

    2011-2013: First La Liga Win and the End of the Mourinho Era .. 35

    2013-2015: La Décima and a 61-goal Season 37

    2015-2018: Three Straight Champions League titles and Ronaldo's Exit from Real Madrid 42

Chapter 5: Juventus 48

2018-2020: Arrival in Italy and Rising to the New Challenge 48

2020-2021 Season: COVID's Impact and Ronaldo's Early Exit from Italy 51

Chapter 6: Return to Manchester United 54

2021 Offseason: A Transfer Saga brings Ronaldo Back to Old Trafford 54

2021-2023: Disappointing Return and Clashes with Erik ten Hag 56

Chapter 7: Al Nassr 59

Chapter 8: International Career 61

2003-2006: Debut and Portugal's 2004 European Championship . 62

2006 World Cup: Becoming Public Enemy Number One in Manchester 64

2007-2011: 2008 Euros, Becoming Portugal's Captain, and the 2010 World Cup 67

2011-2014: 2012 Euros Letdown, Becoming Portugal's Top Scorer, and the 2014 World Cup 71

2015-2016: Winning the 2016 Euros 75

2017-2020: Scoring 100 International Goals for Portugal 80

2020-Present: What's Next 82

Chapter 9: Personal Life 84

Chapter 10: Legacy and Future 88

Final Word/About the Author 93

References 99

Foreword

Ronaldo, a name synonymous with greatness in football, is a Portuguese professional soccer player widely regarded as one of the greatest of all time. Throughout his career, he has graced the fields for some of the most prestigious clubs in the world, including Sporting CP, Manchester United, Real Madrid, Juventus, and currently, Al-Nassr FC. His breakthrough came at Manchester United, where he won three Premier League titles, a UEFA Champions League trophy and his first Ballon d'Or award.

Throughout his career, Ronaldo has won 33 titles, including seven league titles, five UEFA Champions Leagues, a European Championship, and a UEFA Nations League title. His individual accolades are equally impressive, with five Ballon d'Ors, three UEFA Men's Player of the Year awards, and four European Golden Shoes. Ronaldo's success and impact on the sport are undeniable, and he is recognized globally as one of the most accomplished athletes in the world. Thank you for purchasing *Cristiano Ronaldo: The Inspiring Story of One of Soccer's Star Forwards*. In this unauthorized biography, we will learn Cristiano Ronaldo's incredible life story and impact on the game of soccer. Hope you enjoy and if you do, please do not forget to leave a review!

Also, check out my website to join my exclusive list where I let you know about my latest books. To thank you for your purchase, I'll gift you free copies of some of my other books at **claytongeoffreys.com/goodies**.

Or, if you don't like typing, scan the QR code here to go there directly.

Cheers,

Clayton Geoffreys

Visit me at www.claytongeoffreys.com

Introduction

Cristiano Ronaldo dos Santos Aveiro, better known to you and I as Cristiano Ronaldo or just Ronaldo, is one of the greatest soccer players of all time. His power, speed, and technical brilliance allowed him to dominate the world of soccer for over 20 years.

The Portuguese superstar is a five-time Ballon d'Or winner. In total, he has been nominated for the prestigious award, which is given to the best soccer player in the world, a record 18 times.[i] FIFA declared Ronaldo to be the best player in the world on five separate occasions as well.

The former Real Madrid star also earned five Golden Boot awards, which are given to a league's top scorer, in three different leagues. He was awarded the UEFA Golden Shoe award for being Europe's top goal scorer on four occasions. No one has scored more goals for their club than Cristiano Ronaldo has, and no male player has scored more for their country. And these individual awards and records are just the tip of the iceberg when it comes to the individual achievements Ronaldo has won during his illustrious career.

Ronaldo has played a role in some legendary teams at both club and international levels. The now-38-year-old won his first trophy back in 2002 when he was just 17 years old and playing for his boyhood club, Sporting Clube de Portugal (Sporting CP). In the years that followed, Ronaldo won pretty much every trophy there was to win.

With Manchester United emerging as a blossoming global superstar, Ronaldo won the Premier League three times (2006–07, 2007–08, 2008–09), the English FA Cup once (2003–04), the Football League Cup twice (2005–06, 2008–09), the Champions League in 2008, and finally the FIFA Club World Cup, also in 2008.

After achieving all there was to achieve at Manchester United, Ronaldo left England to join another one of the biggest clubs in the world. In 2009, when he was just 24 years old, Ronaldo joined Real Madrid. Los Merengues, a nickname for Real Madrid, paid an astonishing $131.5 million to Man U to secure Ronaldo's signature.[ii] It did not take long for him to prove he was worth that money and a lot more.

Ronaldo brought Real Madrid two La Liga titles (2011–12, 2016–17), two Copas del Rey (2010–11, 2013–14), two Supercopas de España (2012, 2017), and more importantly, four UEFA Champions League titles (2013–14, 2015–16, 2016–17, 2017–18). While at Madrid, Ronaldo also led Portugal to their first and only UEFA European Championship, which they won against France in 2016 with him as team captain.

After making his mark in Madrid and cementing himself as arguably the greatest player of all time, Juventus paid Real Madrid over $117 million to sign Ronaldo in 2018.[iii] He ended up scoring over 100 goals for the Turin-based club and helped them win two Serie A titles, but he could not bring the club the European success that Juventus fans so desperately craved.

Ronaldo left Juve in 2021 and returned to Manchester United. Unfortunately for him and the Red Devils, his second time in England was not as successful as the first. Ronaldo scored 27 goals in 54 matches for Manchester United, but neither he nor the club won any trophies during his one-and-a-half-year spell back in the Premier League. Ronaldo left Manchester again in January 2023, following months of fighting with his coach Erik ten Hag.[iv]

Cristiano now plays for the Saudi Arabian team Al Nassr. While it is not the most glamorous team in the world, Ronaldo's superstar status is still at an all-time high. After Ronaldo came to the Saudi Pro League, dozens of other world-class players followed.[v] Now, many people, including Ronaldo, expect that the Saudi Arabian league will become one of the best leagues in the world in the near future.[vi]

But before all these achievements, before all the money, and before the superstar status, Ronaldo was just a poor child from the city of Funchal on the island of Madeira in Portugal. His journey to the top of the soccer world is one of the most amazing stories in sporting history. It is full of trials and tribulations, with unbelievable highs and devastating lows. To truly see Ronaldo for *all* that he is, we need to start at the beginning.

Chapter 1: Childhood and Early Life

Ronaldo was born on February 5, 1985, in the small Hospital Dr. Nélio Mendonça on the Portuguese island of Madeira.[vii] What happened in the next 38 years is something no one could have predicted.

To understand why it is so surprising that Cristiano Ronaldo ended up where he did, you need to know about his childhood, and that begins with his parents. Both of Ronaldo's parents had an enormous impact on his life, even if his relationship with them was not always close.

Ronaldo's father, José Dinis Aveiro, was born on September 30, 1953. This was a time of upheaval all around the globe. World War II had just ended, European countries were rebuilding and rapidly industrializing, and colonies were demanding independence.

Like many Portuguese men of that era, Aveiro was caught up in that upheaval. Several Portuguese colonies were among the many willing to fight for their independence during these times. On September 4, 1974, Ronaldo's father was forced to go to war against these colonies.[viii]

José Dinis Aveiro, better known simply as Dinis, went to Africa and fought for Portugal in two wars: the Portuguese Colonial War and the Mozambican War of Independence.[ix] At the end of these conflicts, over 100,000 people had died, and José Dinis Aveiro was forever a changed man. When Ronaldo's father returned home from Africa, he brought his memories and wartime experiences back with him.

Dinis struggled to readjust to life back in Portugal. The entire nation was struggling, but life was especially harsh on the islands. When Ronaldo's father came back to the island of Madeira, he quickly found himself in poverty, and subsequently, he turned to alcohol.[viii] Ronaldo's father became an alcoholic who never worked apart from occasional jobs as a gardener and kit man for a local soccer team.[ix] He relied on charity from his friends in order to eat and drink more alcohol.[ix] A bitter, dejected, and angry man, Dinis also often took his rage out on Ronaldo's mother and beat her.[ix]

Before Ronaldo was born, his mother, Maria Dolores dos Santos Viveiros da Aveiro, had already given birth to three of Dinis' children. Because of her family's immense poverty and her partner's alcoholism, Dolores did not want another child.[x] She simply did not have the money or the space for another one. Her three children were already sharing a single bedroom in their small home on the island of Madeira, and she only worked occasionally as a cook and cleaner.

Dolores felt so strongly about not wanting another child that she attempted to get an abortion when she found out she was pregnant with Ronaldo.[xi] Abortions were illegal in Portugal at the time, so she could not get one, but Dolores was desperate. In her autobiography, Ronaldo's mother talks about drinking large amounts of warm ale and running "till she dropped" in order to try and trigger a miscarriage.[xi] Thankfully, her efforts were unsuccessful, and a healthy baby, Cristiano Ronaldo dos Santos Aveiro, was born.

This defenseless baby was born into an incredibly tough situation. His father was an alcoholic whom he could never connect to; his mother did not want him, and both were too poor to take care of him properly. Despite all of this, Ronaldo persevered. Part of the way he persevered was through soccer.

Ronaldo started playing soccer as a young child. When he was just seven years old, he joined a local team in Funchal called CF Andorinha, where his father Dinis was a part-time kit man.[xii]

After three seasons with Andorinha's youth team, Ronaldo moved to the youth academy of a club called Nacional.[xii] Os Nacionalistas, as the club is called by fans, is one of the biggest teams on the island of Madeira where Ronaldo grew up. Even though the team was on the same small island and in the same city where he lived, joining Nacional was a big step up for Ronaldo. However, this was just the beginning.

From Nacional, Ronaldo, a small boy from a poor family on an island in the middle of nowhere, left his home and joined the first "big team" of his career. When he was just twelve years old, Ronaldo left his family, flew to Lisbon on the mainland of Portugal, and joined the Sporting Clube de Portugal youth academy.[xiii] This was a very big change for Ronaldo and his family.

"My siblings and my mother were crying. Even my father was very emotional on that day," said Ronaldo of the day he left Madeira for Lisbon.[xiv] Ronaldo was also very emotional. "I cried every day because I missed my family."[xiv]

The Sporting CP Academy was one of the best and most intense and competitive youth soccer environments in the world. Youth players lived together in dorms, called residencies.[ix] They received traditional schooling from Sporting CP, but otherwise, their entire lives revolved around football. Many of the kids there were poor, just like Ronaldo. They could not afford to buy food for themselves outside of what the club would give them, so they would go and beg for old burgers at a McDonald's near their residency.[ix]

If Ronaldo was going to make it from the residency and become a first team player, he would have to fight, put in the necessary hard work, and shine above the rest of his youth teammates. This was something Ronaldo had been doing for his entire young life, so, of course he was able to do it again as a Sporting CP Academy player. He did it so quickly, in fact, that other Sporting CP Academy players immediately knew Ronaldo was going to be great.

"There were many footballers with plenty of talent [in the Sporting CP Academy], but Cristiano had something special. He had different things. He was never satisfied with the amount he did. He always wanted more" said Miguel Paixão, one of Ronaldo's close friends whom he met playing at the Sporting CP Academy.[xiv]

Jose Semedo, another player in the Sporting CP Academy with Ronaldo, described Ronaldo's first training session with Sporting as something he had never seen before.[xiv] Semedo said, "[Ronaldo] was so much better than everybody. So, so much better."[xiv]

Ronaldo's skills also impressed his coaches. After just four years as an academy player, he was invited to the Sporting CP first team by the club's manager, Ladislau (László) Boloni.[xv] The Romanian coach was awed by Ronaldo's dribbling ability and ability to do impressive tricks with the ball.

"I couldn't stop him from dribbling and other tricks," said Boloni.[xv]

As we would see in future years, neither could Ronaldo's opponents.

Chapter 2: Sporting CP Senior Team

Cristiano Ronaldo's journey to becoming a professional soccer player was long, winding, and full of hardship. His path to becoming a first team player for Sporting CP after graduating from the Sporting Academy could not have been more different, however.

In 2002, Ronaldo progressed from the Under-16 team to the Senior team in just one season. He was the first player in club history to play in Sporting's Under-16, Under-17, Under-18, B-team, and Senior teams all within a single season.[xvi] To put into perspective how big an achievement this is, it can often take a player five years or more to progress through those same teams. Ronaldo did it in just a few months.

The biggest leap forward for Ronaldo during the 2002-2003 season was when he went from the Under-18 to Sporting's B team. European football teams often have reserve teams to help integrate their players from the youth teams to the first team. The other effect these reserve teams have is helping the clubs identify which players are ready to play with grown men, as opposed to playing with other kids in the youth teams. Many players get promoted to the B team and then get sent right back down to the youth teams because they are not physically or mentally prepared for high-level professional football. This was not the case with Ronaldo, who joined the Sporting B team and never looked back.

Ronaldo started training with the Sporting B team ahead of the 2002-2003 season. He impressed his coaches so much at that level that he was asked to train with the first team. A 17-year-old Ronaldo was even included in Sporting's squad for the 2002 Supertaça Cândido de Oliveira. This competition is a single-game event played at the start of the season between last year's league champions and national cup winners. Ronaldo never left the bench in this game, but his team won, meaning that Ronaldo got the very first winner's medal of his illustrious career.

Ronaldo made his professional debut just one month after his team's Supertaça Cândido de Oliveira victory. The 17-year-old came on for Sporting B in a 2-1 loss to Sport Clube Lusitânia. He did not have much of an impact on that game, but still proved to his coaches that he was already too good to be playing B-team soccer. Ronaldo would play just one more game with the B team before becoming a full member of Sporting CP's senior team.

On September 29, 2002, less than a month after his B-team debut, Ronaldo made his debut for the Sporting CP first team.

He came on briefly as a substitute for Sporting in the 68th minute of a match against Braga. Sporting were already down 4-2 in the match when Ronaldo came on. He was unable to make an impact, and 4-2 is how the match ended. Just one week later, though, the world would finally see what Cristiano Ronaldo was all about.

In his club's very next game after their 4-2 defeat to Braga, Ronaldo was named in the starting lineup for the first time in his Sporting career. Sporting were playing Moreirense in a match at home, so this game was also the first time thousands of Sporting fans were able to see their new wonderkid in action. Starting debuts like this rarely live up to the hype, but Ronaldo's did. The 17-year-old winger scored two goals and helped his Sporting team secure a 3-0 win over Moreirense in front of their adoring fans.

Ronaldo shone bright in his first appearance, but he did not get many more goals throughout the rest of his first season as a professional soccer player. He played 24 of Sporting's final 17 league games, but only scored one more goal and had just three assists. Despite this being the case, Ronaldo's talent was clear to see for anyone watching.

Ronaldo was thus linked to a number of huge European soccer clubs that were interested in acquiring him, including Barcelona, Liverpool, and Arsenal. The former two of those three clubs were apparently never real options. Liverpool's manager at the time, Gerard Houllier, later said that the Reds "went for [Ronaldo], but we had a wage scale and we weren't paying the sort of salary he wanted."[xvii]

Barcelona also rejected Ronaldo, but it was not because of wages. The Catalan club had just signed legendary Brazilian player Ronaldinho and Ronaldo's Sporting teammate Ricardo Quaresma, so they did not have a place for him in their team.[xviii]

As for Arsenal, they were "very close" to signing him, according to Ronaldo himself.[ix] Former Arsenal manager Arsene Wenger later called not signing Ronaldo his biggest regret.[xix] The team that ultimately won out and secured the rising football star's signature was Manchester United.

Sir Alex Ferguson saw firsthand what Ronaldo could do in a preseason match between Manchester United and Sporting CP. The legendary Scotsman watched the then-18-year-old Ronaldo and his Sporting teammates beat Manchester United 3-1. According to Houllier, who knew Sir Alex well, Man U players were saying to Ferguson after the match "'You have to sign him." [xvii]

The former Manchester United manager has never confirmed this story, but if you listen to what the Red Devils players who played that night have to say, the story seems very believable.

"It was an incredible performance to watch that night," said former Manchester United defender and France national team player Mikael Silvestre. "This kid nobody knew tore us apart for the whole game. No one could get near him; he was amazing."[xx]

After Ronaldo's incredible performance, Sir Alex Ferguson had to have him. Manchester United beat out every other big team chasing Ronaldo and signed him for £12.24 million. This was the most a British team had ever paid for a teenage player. At the time, Ferguson called Ronaldo "one of the most exciting young players I've ever seen."[xxi]

It did not take long for Cristiano Ronaldo to prove that Ferguson was right and that he was worth every pound Manchester United had spent on him.

Chapter 3: Manchester United

2003-2006: Slow Start and Developmental Years

Ronaldo's rise at Sporting CP cannot be described as anything but meteoric. His time at Manchester United, on the other hand, was more of a slow burn.

The 18-year-old winger joined the Red Devils just before their first game of the 2003-2004 season. Manchester United had finished the previous season as Premier League champions and were widely regarded as one of the biggest and best teams in the world. Under any circumstances, joining such a big club would come with a lot of pressure. For Ronaldo, the pressure was even greater than it would be for a normal player. This was because of his manager, Sir Alex Ferguson.

Fergie, as Sir Alex Ferguson was affectionately called, turned the pressure up even more on Ronaldo by giving him the No. 7 jersey. This jersey number is a legendary one at Manchester United. Icons like George Best, Bryan Robson, and Eric Cantona have all worn that number for Manchester United.

Best, an undisputed club legend and one of the most important players in United's history, reflected on Ronaldo getting his old number. "There have been a few players described as 'the new

George Best' over the years, but this is the first time it's been a compliment to me. There have been players who have some similarities, but this lad's got more than anyone else."[xxii] This was immense praise from a genuine legend, but for Ronaldo, the most important Manchester United player to have worn No. 7 was David Beckham.

Becks, as the media often called David Beckham, had left Manchester United to join Real Madrid just before Ronaldo signed with United. Not only was Beckham one of soccer's biggest global superstars but he was also one of Manchester United's best players. Beckham's shoes were big ones to fill, and everyone was expecting Ronaldo to fill them right away. But, unfortunately for him and for Manchester United fans, they would have to wait a few years for Ronaldo to reach the heights that David Beckham did with Manchester United.

It took Ronaldo two seasons to get as many combined league goals and assists as David Beckham had in his final Manchester United season. Furthermore, the club was not successful on the field. In the three seasons prior to Ronaldo's arrival at the club, Manchester United had won the league twice and never got knocked out of the Champions League earlier than the quarterfinals. In Ronaldo's first three seasons with United, the club's only silverware was a single FA Cup win. In the

Champions League, the club was knocked out in the Round of 16 twice and in the Group Stage on one occasion.

While neither Ronaldo nor his team were particularly stellar during his first three seasons with them, the signs were clearly there that Ronaldo would soon become the global superstar we now know today.

Ronaldo's goal tally steadily improved every year at Manchester United during his first three seasons. He scored just four goals in his first season, five in his second, and finally, nine goals in his third season.

Besides the goals, Ronaldo was looking more and more comfortable as a Premier League player. Defenders began to fear Ronaldo when he had the ball on the wing and when he stood over free kicks. It was no surprise, then, when Ronaldo finally put it all together in his fourth season with Manchester United. Before that breakout fourth season, though, Ronaldo played in the 2006 World Cup and nearly derailed his career doing so.

2006-2007 Season: World Cup Drama and Breakout Season

Prior to the 2006-2007 season, Ronaldo became one of the most hated players in England thanks to his actions at the 2006 World Cup. At that tournament, Portugal, Ronaldo's national team, and England faced off in the quarterfinals.

It was a very intense game—so intense, in fact, that Wayne Rooney, Ronaldo's Manchester United teammate, was given a red card and ejected from the match for stepping on the groin of Portugal's Ricardo Carvalho during a battle for the ball. Ronaldo was then blamed for Rooney's being sent off since he was seen pleading with the referee and asking him to give the Englishman a red card. Ronaldo was also caught on camera winking at Rooney as he walked off the pitch.

These actions created a very hostile environment for Ronaldo back in Manchester. It got so bad that he wanted to leave the club before the 2006-2007 season.[xxiii] Thankfully for Manchester United fans, however, the club was unwilling to sell Ronaldo. The wonderkid stayed in Manchester and subsequently had the best season of his career so far.

The 2006-2007 season was Ronaldo's fourth season in Manchester. It also was his first season as one of Manchester

United's main men. Ronaldo, and his controversial "frenemy" from the summer incident, Wayne Rooney, led the Red Devils back to the top of English soccer.

Ronaldo scored 17 league goals and 23 overall for his club. This was more than anyone else on the team and third-most in the Premier League that season. But more important than those individual accolades, the 2006-2007 season was Ronaldo's first league win with Manchester United. The Red Devils finished at the top of the Premier League by a wide margin. They earned 89 points. The next best team was Chelsea with just 83 points. Behind them was Liverpool, Manchester United's biggest rival, who could only muster 68 points on the season.

Manchester United also had domestic cup success. They made it all the way to the final of the 2006-2007 FA Cup before getting knocked out by Chelsea in the final. Ronaldo made seven appearances in the competition and scored three goals.

In addition to domestic success, Manchester United and Ronaldo also experienced new highs together in Europe's top continental competition. In the 2006-2007 season, Manchester United went further in the Champions League than they had in Ronaldo's previous three seasons with the club. The Red Devils advanced all the way to the Champions League semifinal. This was the furthest they had progressed in that competition since the 2001-2002 season.

Ronaldo played a big role in the club's re-found Champions League success. The winger's most notable performance came in United's 7-1 thrashing of Roma where he scored twice. He also scored two goals against AC Milan in the first leg of the Semifinal, although he was unable to score in the second leg and Manchester United was knocked out of the tournament.

At the end of the season, Ronaldo was named the English Professional Footballers' Association's Player's Player of the Season, the PFA Fans' Player of the Year, Young Player of the Year, and the Football Writers Association's Footballer of the Year. He was also among the top three Ballon d'Or vote-getters for the first time in his career. Ronaldo finished second in Ballon d'Or voting, just behind Brazil and Milan's Kaká.

2007-2008 Season: Rise to Global Superstardom

As good as Ronaldo's 2006-2007 season was, his 2007-2008 campaign was even better. If the 2006-2007 season was the year when Ronaldo established himself as the best player in England, the 2007-2008 campaign was where he proved to everyone that he was one of the best players in the world.

Ronaldo started this season rather slowly. He headbutted a Portsmouth player in the first match of the season and had to sit out the next three games. After serving his suspension, it took Ronaldo a little longer to score. He did not get his first league goal for Manchester United until the eighth game of the season. Once he did score, though, he did not stop.

Ronaldo scored a phenomenal 42 goals in all competitions for Manchester United in the 2007-2008 season, 31 of which came in the Premier League. No Manchester United player before or after has scored as many goals in the Premier League as Ronaldo did in this season. It goes without saying, then, that the Portuguese superstar was his team's leading goal scorer that season. He was also the Premier League's top scorer, and more importantly, the top goal scorer in the Champions League.

Thanks to Ronaldo's goal-scoring, Manchester United was able to do what few teams in football history have ever done— United won the Premier League *and* the Champions League in the same season.

The former of these achievements looked tight at times, as Manchester United had to fight off Chelsea and Arsenal to secure their 10th Premier League title. Ronaldo scored key goals late on in the season against Wigan Athletic and West

Ham United which ultimately secured Manchester United's championship.

While winning the Premier League had looked difficult at times for United, it could not have been more different in the Champions League. Manchester United did not lose a single match in the 2007-2008 Champions League. To emphasize just how dominant the Red Devils were in this competition, they gave up just 6 goals total in their 13 Champions League matches. Ronaldo scored eight goals by himself in the Champions League.

The only match where things had looked really dicey for Manchester United was the final against Chelsea. Ronaldo scored in the 26th minute to put United up 1-0 early, but things never felt comfortable for them.

Before the goal, both sides had been playing in a very contentious manner. It was clear that neither team wanted to be the first one to make a mistake. Neither team ended up doing so, but Chelsea still ended up getting on the scoreboard just before half-time. It was 1-1 going into the second half, and that was what the score stayed at for the rest of the match. The game then went to penalties, where uncharacteristically, Ronaldo missed his penalty. Thankfully, the winger's teammates had his back.

Every other Red Devils player scored. Thus, Manchester United were the Champions League champions for the third time in their history.

For his efforts in the 2007-2008 season, Ronaldo again won the PFA Young Player of the Year, PFA Players' Player of the Year, PFA Fans' Player of the Year, Football Writers Association Footballer of the Year, and Premier League Player of the Season. In addition to those accolades, Ronaldo also won his first Ballon d'Or, FIFA Player of the Year, UEFA Club Footballer of the Year, and the European Golden Shoe Award.

Despite all his incredible success on the pitch, Ronaldo was not happy at Manchester United. At this point in his career, Real Madrid were desperate to sign Ronaldo, and he was desperate to join them. In fact, Madrid's tactics to sign the Ballon d'Or winner were so extreme that Manchester United filed a formal tampering complaint with FIFA against the Spanish club.[xxiv] FIFA emphatically dismissed Manchester United's complaint with then FIFA President Sepp Blatter, calling United's wish to keep Ronaldo "modern slavery."[xxv]

After Portugal was knocked out in the quarterfinals of the 2008 Euros, Ronaldo came out again to publicly request a transfer from Manchester United. He agreed with Blatter that his current situation was like slavery.

"I agree with what [Blatter] said," Ronaldo responded when asked by reporters about Blatter's comments.[xxvi] But once again, Ronaldo's discontent and pleas for his freedom fell on deaf ears. The Portuguese superstar would stay at Manchester United for another season.

2008-2009: Ronaldo's Final Season at Manchester United

Ronaldo started the 2008-2009 season amid controversy about his failed transfer to Real Madrid. He also started it at home thanks to an injury. In July of 2008, Ronaldo underwent ankle surgery to correct an injury he suffered at the end of the prior season which was then aggravated at the 2008 Euros.[xxvi] In total, Ronaldo missed 10 weeks of soccer. However, because the surgery was so early in the summer, he only had to miss one league game for Manchester United.

Once he was focused back on Manchester United instead of Real Madrid, Ronaldo had another strong season for the Red Devils. He finished the year with 26 goals across all competitions and was again Manchester United's leading scorer.

He was also a Premier League champion with the Manchester club for the second straight year.

The club earned 90 points, which was more than they had ever gotten with Ronaldo previously. Manchester United also won the League Cup for just the third time in their history. In many other years, Manchester United might have been Champions League champions again. Yet, despite this domestic dominance, they could not repeat their success in the Champions League. But it was not for lack of trying.

Like they had in the previous season, Manchester United went undefeated in the Champions League. Well, to be more specific, they were undefeated until the final match.

Manchester United managed another stellar campaign in which they gave up just five goals in their first 12 games. Ronaldo scored four goals in those 12 matches, but, like the rest of his team, he could not score in the final. The Red Devils lost 2-0 to Barcelona at Rome's Stadio Olimpico in the 2009 Champions League. This would be Ronaldo's last match for Manchester United—for a while at least.

After six seasons in Manchester, it was time for something different. In Ronaldo's own words, "I wanted more. I wanted another league. I wanted a different kind of football. I wanted a different chapter, a different challenge in my life."[xiv]

The young superstar would find everything he was looking for and more when he joined Real Madrid in the summer of 2009.

Chapter 4: Real Madrid

2009-2011: Headlining Real Madrid's Second Galácticos Era

Real Madrid is arguably the biggest football club in the world. They earned this sterling reputation not only for their successes on the field but also because Real Madrid has a long history of signing the most famous players in the world.

This trend started all the way back in the 1950s, when the Madrid-based club signed legendary Argentine striker Alfredo Di Stéfano and Hungarian superstar Ferenc Puskás. Real Madrid continued this tradition under new president Florentino Pérez in the early 2000s when the club signed players like Luís Figo, Brazilian Ronaldo, Zinedine Zidane, and David Beckham.

These Pérez-era signings were known as Galácticos. Unfortunately for Pérez, these signings did not always result in strong on-field performances. Florentino Pérez resigned from his position as Real Madrid President in 2006. However, he soon returned in 2009 and restarted his infamous Galácticos policy. Signing Cristiano Ronaldo was essential to Pérez's "Second Galácticos" era.

Real Madrid signed Ronaldo for €94 million (roughly $101 million U.S.), which was a world record transfer fee at the time.[ii] Over 80,000 excited Madridistas welcomed Ronaldo at the Estadio Santiago Bernabéu.[xxvii]

"I felt like a star, like a pop star or a Hollywood star," Ronaldo said of having nearly 90,000 people come to Real Madrid's stadium to see him for the first time.[xiv] "For me, I've achieved my childhood dream, which was to play for Real Madrid," he said at his unveiling.[xiv]

In the following years, these same Real Madrid fans would welcome numerous other Galácticos to the club, like Gareth Bale, Karim Benzema, Luka Modrić, and Toni Kroos. These players would not only be a part of Pérez's "Second Galácticos" but also some of the most successful soccer players in the world. Expectations were high for this group, and everyone knew it.

"I knew that after Real Madrid signed me that the pressure would mount," said Ronaldo. "Real Madrid wanted to win the Champions League, and obviously, to win, you need to have the best players."[xiv]

Real Madrid had done the first part. They had signed some of the best players in the world. However, winning the Champions

League and other team successes would not come immediately for Ronaldo at Real Madrid.

In Ronaldo's first season in Spain, the 2009-10 season, he scored 33 goals. This was more than any other player at Real Madrid. His 26 league goals were only bettered by Gonzalo Higuaín and Lionel Messi in La Liga. As impressive as these numbers are, they could have been better. Ronaldo suffered an ankle injury midway through the season that sidelined him for seven weeks.[xxviii] This injury stopped him from scoring goals. It also stopped Real Madrid from achieving anything during Ronaldo's first season at the club. The 2009-2010 season would be the only one during the Portuguese superstar's time at the club when he did not win a trophy.

Ronaldo's second season, the 2010-11 season, was much more successful for him and Real Madrid. It was this season when Ronaldo would establish himself as more than just a great player but also as one of the best players to ever play soccer.

He scored 51 goals for Real Madrid in the 2010-11 season. Scoring more than 50 goals in a season is something only the greatest players in history have done, so Ronaldo had put himself in elite company by scoring that many goals. For his efforts as a goal scorer, Ronaldo was awarded the European

Golden Shoe, which is given to Europe's top goal scorer, for the second time in his career.

In addition to scoring goals and winning personal accolades, the 2010-11 season was also the first time Ronaldo put his name in the Real Madrid history books for helping the club win the Copa del Rey. This trophy is one of the most important in Spain, so it was a momentous achievement for Ronaldo and his new club. But while this trophy is definitely a big deal, the 2010-11 season is best known for Real Madrid's many battles with their bitter rivals, Barcelona.

Real Madrid and Barcelona were drawn against each other in the Champions League. This is something that rarely ever happens. But if you were a soccer fan at the time, you were incredibly happy that it did happen because this Champions League draw resulted in one of the most iconic three weeks in soccer history.

Over the course of 18 days between April 16th and May 3, 2011, Real Madrid and Barcelona played each other four times. So many Clásico matches had never occurred in such a small period of time. However, what makes these matches iconic is not just that they happened so soon after each other. The 2011 Clásico matches are forever remembered for being some of the most intense rivalries ever played. Of course, Ronaldo played a big role in why they were so intense.

The first match of this series was a league match that ended in a 1-1 draw. Both Ronaldo and Messi scored, and an astonishing eight players were given yellow or red cards.

The next match was even more spectacular because of the stakes involved. The second Clásico of the four in 18 days was the 2011 Copa del Rey final. This match was equally as brutal as the first. Eight players were again given cards, and it ended in a 0-0 draw, meaning that it went to extra time. Ronaldo scored the winning goal in the 103rd minute at Estadio de Mestalla in Valencia.

The third and fourth matches of this streak were unfortunately not as kind to Madrid, and they were even more violent. Ronaldo and Real Madrid were knocked out of the Champions League by Barcelona. Both clubs were embroiled in controversy over physical altercations on the field and the sidelines during these matches.

In total, Barcelona would win just one of these four iconic Clásico matches, but they would have the last laugh in the end by narrowly beating Real Madrid to the 2011 La Liga title.

However, Barca would not be able to repeat their title in the following year.

2011-2013: First La Liga Win and the End of the Mourinho Era

The 2011-12 season, Ronaldo's third season at Real Madrid, was another one for the history books. The superstar striker scored 60 goals, seven more than he had in the prior year. As a team, this 2011-12 Real Madrid squad were known by many simply as the "Record Breakers" because they broke several La Liga records that many thought would remain unbroken for eternity.

The 2011-12 Real Madrid team broke the records for most wins (32), most away wins (16), most goals (121), and best goal difference in a season (+89). But perhaps the most impressive record this incredible team set was most points in a season. The 2011-12 Real Madrid team was the first team in La Liga history to earn 100 points. The prior record was 99 points, which was set by Barcelona in the 2009-10 season, Ronaldo's first season in Spain. Setting this record also obviously meant that Real Madrid won La Liga—Ronaldo's first league title in Madrid and the most prestigious trophy he had won for Real Madrid so far.

While Real Madrid were record breakers in the 2011-12 season, Ronaldo was not. In any other year, Ronaldo's 46 league goals would have been enough to break the record for most goals scored by an individual in a La Liga season. But, unfortunately for Ronaldo, the 2011-12 season was also Messi's most prolific season, and the most prolific season in soccer history. The little Argentine scored 50 league goals and 73 for his club overall. Because both players had such legendary seasons, many consider this season to be the peak of the Messi vs. Ronaldo rivalry.

Messi would get the upper hand again in the 2012-13 season when he scored 46 league goals compared to Ronaldo's 34. The Argentine's team, Barcelona, would also regain control of the La Liga title in the 2012-13 season. Real Madrid finished second in the league that year with just 85 points, 15 points behind Barcelona. The club's only trophy win that year came in the Supercopa de España, which was the least prestigious trophy Real Madrid could have won that season.

By Real Madrid's high standards, the 2012-13 season was simply atrocious. It was so bad that their manager, José Mourinho, was fired by club president Florentino Pérez at the end of the season. For Ronaldo, though, the 2012-13 season was one of his best ever.

Because his Real Madrid team was so bad, Ronaldo was forced to do everything. In 2015, Ronaldo said the 2012-13 season was the "best year of my career. Without any doubt."[xiv] Ronaldo won the Ballon d'Or in 2013 and 2014 for his efforts in this season. This would likely be the peak of most players' careers, but Ronaldo? He was just getting started!

2013-2015: La Décima and a 61-goal Season

In Ronaldo's first four years at Real Madrid, he and his club won one league title, one Copa del Rey, and a Supercopa de España. In addition to those three trophies, Ronaldo scored over 200 goals during that period. For any other player, at any other club, these achievements would have been considered glowing successes. However, they were not perceived that way for Ronaldo and Real Madrid. Why? Because Ronaldo is not a normal player, and Real Madrid is not a normal football club.

At Real Madrid, you cannot be considered a club legend unless you win the Champions League. It does not matter how many goals you score, how many Ballon d'Ors you win, or how many league titles you win. The Champions League is all that matters. It's like the Super Bowl of American football.

Ronaldo's previous manager, Jose Mourinho, was brought in with a reputation as a tournament specialist. He had previously led Porto to one of the most unlikely Champions League victories in history. Unfortunately for Ronaldo and Real Madrid, Mourinho could not get the job done in Spain and was sacked ahead of the 2013-14 La Liga season. Carlo Ancelotti was hired to be his replacement.

Ancelotti was another title specialist. Despite Mourinho being known as the "Special One," Ancelotti's reputation was even greater.[xxix] He had won more Champions League titles than Mourinho, including the two he won as a player. The biggest difference between the two managers was that Ancelotti was less of an abrasive personality than Mourinho. Unlike many of the greatest managers of the 21st Century, Carlo Ancelotti did not have a strict tactical plan that he imposed on his squads. The legendary Italian manager is better known as a "man" manager than a tactician. He has even admitted so on multiple occasions.

"The important thing is the relationships you have with other people. I'm with my players every day—actually, it's not right to call them my players. I'm with my friends every day. Because there's the player and then there's the person," said Ancelotti to Spanish media ahead of the 2022 Champions League.[xxx]

For Ronaldo, this managerial approach was perfect. Instead of being forced into an already-defined system, Ancelotti would create a system that allowed Ronaldo to do what he did best. This resulted in the greatest achievement of the Portuguese superstar's career.

In Ancelotti's first season at Real Madrid, Ronaldo scored 51 goals in just 47 games. Furthermore, 17 of these goals came in the Champions League, which is the record for most goals scored by a single player in one CL campaign. More important than all the goals he scored, though, was what his team accomplished. Ronaldo finally got his Champions League title with Real Madrid. And it was not any Champions League in either. It was La Décima.

La Décima, otherwise known as Real Madrid's 10th Champions League win, is arguably the most important one in club history. Part of the reason for this is because it took so long to achieve. Real Madrid won the first five Champions Leagues ever, spanning the period of 1955-1960. They won their sixth just six years later in 1966. However, it would take another 32 years for Real Madrid to get their seventh Champions League title. They would get their eighth and ninth two and four years after their fourth, respectively. After winning their ninth, Real Madrid fell off as a participant in the Champions League.

Real Madrid did not feature in a Champions League final between 2002, when they won their ninth title, and 2014. This 12-year gap from finals appearances was the longest in the history of Real Madrid since the 1980s. But winning La Décima changed all that. It also catapulted Cristiano Ronaldo to even greater heights than he had achieved in his career up to that point.

Ronaldo was awarded the 2013 Ballon d'Or in January 2014. He was also given the 2014 award for his record-breaking Champions League campaign that helped Madrid win La Décima. This accomplishment makes him just one of seven players who have been awarded the Ballon d'Or in consecutive seasons.

As good as Ronaldo's 2013-14 season was, he topped it in 2014-15. In this season, he scored 61 goals. To put that number in perspective, only four players have ever scored more goals than that in a season. Two of those four players, Dixie Dean and Ferenc Deak, played during the pre-1950 period of football before it was professionalized. The other two top all-time goal scorers are Lionel Messi, who, of course, scored a ridiculous 72 goals in the 2011-12 season, and Gerd Muller, a legendary German striker. These iconic players are who Ronaldo could now compare himself to. Unfortunately for the Real Madrid player, goals were about the only thing he could celebrate in the 2014-15 season.

Real Madrid did not win La Liga, the Champions League, or even the Copa del Rey during the 2014-15 campaign. To make matters worse, their bitter rivals, Barcelona, won a much-lauded treble by winning all three—La Liga, the Copa del Rey, and Champions League. Lionel Messi did not score as many goals as Ronaldo did during this season but his team accomplishments earned him the 2015 Ballon d'Or over Ronaldo regardless.

It is hard to overstate just how disappointing the 2014-15 season was for Real Madrid as a team. The club's legacy of winning many Champions Leagues is very well known. What fewer people realize is that Real Madrid tends to win their Champions League titles in spurts. They won their first five in five consecutive seasons. Titles seven, eight, and nine came within a five-year period as well.

So, after the triumph of La Décima, many fans expected Real Madrid to go on a similar run of Champions League titles, like they did in the 1950s and at the turn of the century.

Ronaldo even commented on the optimism of Real Madrid fans. "[In Spain], I can single out their optimism and the way they value all that they have."[xxxi]

Given this optimism, the disappointment of the 2014-15 season, combined with the extreme success of Barcelona, crushed many Real Madrid fans' hopes and dreams. Thankfully, they would not have to wait long for that dream. However, there would be painful moments along the way.

2015-2018: Three Straight Champions League titles and Ronaldo's Exit from Real Madrid

Legendary manager Carlo Ancelotti left the team before the 2015-16 season, Ronaldo's seventh season with Real Madrid. Ancelotti was replaced by Rafael Benítez. Like Ancelotti, Benítez had previously won the Champions League. In fact, he had actually defeated Ancelotti in the 2005 UEFA Champions League final when his Liverpool side completed an amazing three-goal comeback in the second half, which forced the match into penalties.

But, while Benítez had a resume as impressive as Ancelotti's, he was a very different kind of manager. Unlike Ancelotti, who prioritized developing a good relationship with his players, keeping them happy, and playing a system that suited their strengths, Benítez asked Real Madrid to play *his* style. Benítez's signature style prioritizes defense first, so you could perhaps understand why a player like Cristiano Ronaldo was not performing as well under Benítez as he was under Ancelotti.

Despite his relatively poor performances under Benítez, the 2015-16 season was still a monumental one for Ronaldo. The Portuguese legend scored a remarkable five goals against Espanyol early in the season. His fifth and final goal in that match made him Real Madrid's top goal scorer ever, passing his old teammate Raul's record.[xxxii]

A few weeks later, Ronaldo would break the club's overall goal-scoring record and score his 500th career goal.[xxxiii] Looking back in hindsight, these are two records that will probably never be broken. But, at the time, they were nothing more than lipstick on a pig. This was because every Real Madrid player, not just Ronaldo, was struggling under Benítez's new soccer system. Ultimately, these struggles cost Benítez his job. The Spanish manager was fired on January 4, 2016.[xxxiv] He was replaced by Real Madrid legend Zinedine Zidane.[xxxv]

For those unfamiliar with the dynamics of football management, when a big-name manager is replaced by a lower member of his staff or by a former player, it almost never goes well. These interim managers become just that, *interim*. They almost never become permanent managers. This was not the case with Zidane, however. Not only did the French World Cup winner become the permanent Real Madrid manager but he also went on to become one of the greatest managers of the 21st Century. How did he do it? He did it by letting players like Ronaldo play.

Zidane comes from the same school of coaching as Ancelotti. He viewed his job as keeping his players happy and putting them into positions where they would be successful. Zidane did this brilliantly, and with immediate effect.

Madrid won their first game under their new manager 5-0. They won their second match 5-1, a game against Sporting Gijon in which Ronaldo scored twice. In total, Real Madrid lost just 2 of their remaining 27 matches in the 2015-16 season after Zidane took charge. Ronaldo scored 24 goals in those 27 matches.

Neither Ronaldo nor Zidane's efforts in the second half of the season were rewarded with a league title. Real Madrid finished second in the league, behind Barcelona again. However, this was okay, because Ronaldo and Madrid won something even better. Once the shackles were let off Ronaldo and his teammates, they marched along to yet another Champions League title. This was their second title in three years, but it was just the beginning of the Ronaldo, Zidane, Karim Benzema, and Gareth Bale era at Real Madrid.

In the 2016-17 season, Ronaldo scored just 42 goals. This was the fewest number he had scored since the 2009-10 season, his first at Real Madrid (and which was also plagued by injuries). But while his goal-scoring was down, no one was complaining. Bale and Benzema were scoring plenty of goals as well, so the team did not need to rely solely on Ronaldo like they had in the past.

More importantly, the team was winning. The 2016-17 Real Madrid team won every competition they played in except for the Copa del Rey. Los Merengues won La Liga, the UEFA Super Cup, FIFA Club World Cup, and the Champions League. Their Champions League win was against Juventus, which will be important later in Ronaldo's story.

For these accomplishments as an individual and as a part of the Real Madrid teams who had won back-to-back Champions Leagues, Ronaldo was again awarded two straight Ballon d'Or awards in 2016 and 2017. The achievements and accolades would not stop coming for Ronaldo and Real Madrid.

In the very next season, Real Madrid would do it all again. The Madridistas won the Supercopa de España, UEFA Super Cup, FIFA Club World Cup, and, of course, the Champions League. This third straight Champions League victory, their fourth win in five seasons, cemented the 2013-2018 Real Madrid team as one of the best in football history. It also cemented Ronaldo's status as one of the greatest players to ever play the game.

Between 2013 and 2018, Ronaldo scored more goals than any other player in the Champions League during that period. If we zoom out just a little, Ronaldo won the UEFA Champions League top scorer award every year between 2012 and 2018. He also won the European Golden Boot in two of those years. Ronaldo also won four Ballon d'Or awards for being the best player in the world during this period.

Simply put, Ronaldo reached levels few footballers have ever reached. And he was rewarded for it with numerous personal accolades and team success on the pitch in multiple competitions, including the Champions League. When someone reaches the highest echelons of a sport like this, it is hard to imagine them coming down, but that is exactly what happened to Ronaldo immediately following the 2018 Champions League Final against Liverpool.

In his post-match comments, Ronaldo repeatedly referred to his time playing in Madrid in the past tense, which led many to think that he would be leaving the club soon.[xxxv] After months of speculation and contract negotiations, Ronaldo confirmed everyone's suspicions.[xxxvi] That Champions League final against Liverpool was Ronaldo's last match for Real Madrid. On July 10, 2018, Juventus signed Ronaldo, luring him away from Real Madrid for €100m.[xxxvii]

Chapter 5: Juventus

2018-2020: Arrival in Italy and Rising to the New Challenge

Before Ronaldo's shocking post-match comments about leaving Madrid, no one ever imagined him leaving the club, so when he did, people went looking for answers. After all, Ronaldo was at the top of the mountain with Real Madrid. Why would he walk away?

In his own words, he wanted to challenge himself in another league because had accomplished all there was to do in Spain.[xxxviii] Or in other words, he had conquered La Liga. Serie A was next.

When Ronaldo joined Juventus, they were the best team in Italy. Prior to his arrival, they had won seven straight Serie A titles and four straight Coppa Italia competitions.

Despite joining such a highly lauded team, moving to a new country can be a challenge for anyone. For a soccer player like Ronaldo, it meant adopting and adjusting to the league's different play style, your new teammates, the different venues, different media climate, and so much more. So, even though Juve was a dominant club, conquering Italy like he did Spain would not be a cakewalk for Ronaldo. Proof of this came in his first few matches with Juventus.

Ronaldo did not score until his fourth match with the club, when he bagged two goals against Sassuolo in a 2-1 Juventus victory. In his fifth match for the Old Lady, as Juventus is often called, Ronaldo picked up a red card. This was his first-ever red card in the Champions League, and ironically, it came against a Spanish team, Valencia.

The rest of the 2018-19 season went similarly for Ronaldo at Juventus. He would score a few goals, then go on a cold streak. For most players, this is normal. For Ronaldo, it was cause for major concern. Plus, he was 35 years old at the end of the season. This is when most players start to slow down, and exactly what we saw from Ronaldo. He only scored 28 goals. The last time he scored such a small number of goals was when he was playing for Manchester United. Thus, people were worried, including the brass at his new club.

Juventus did not need Cristiano Ronaldo to win Serie A, which they did easily in the 2018-19 season with him at the club. They signed him to help them get over the hump in the Champions League. Ronaldo had knocked out Juventus in the Champions League on multiple occasions, including once with a spectacular bicycle kick volley. Juventus were thus hoping that Ronaldo would bring his own talent and some of Real Madrid's winning DNA to help them win their first Champions League since 1996.

Unfortunately for them, Ronaldo could not get the job done in year one. He scored just six Champions League goals and Juventus was ultimately knocked out in the quarterfinals by Ajax, who were massive underdogs. Ronaldo scored Juventus's only two goals in that tie.

His second season in Turin with Juventus did not go much better. Yes, Ronaldo scored more goals. He upped his tally from 28 in all competitions to 37. However, his production in the Champions League still went down. He scored just four Champions League goals. Part of the reason for this was because Juventus played fewer Champions League games in the 2019-20 season. They were then knocked out of the Round of 16 again by an underdog. This time it was Lyon.

While they could not get it done in Europe, Juventus again won Serie A, proving they were the best team in Italy for the ninth straight season.

2020-2021 Season: COVID's Impact and Ronaldo's Early Exit from Italy

2020 will be remembered for a lot of things, but the thing that people will remember most is the onset of the COVID-19 pandemic. On March 9, 2020, Italy suspended all sporting events, including soccer.[xxxix] Players would be off and away from their clubs for over two months, and the season would not resume until June 20, 2020.[xl] COVID-19's impact did not stop Juventus from winning the 2019-20 Serie A title. However, it would have a major impact on their 2020-21 season, and on Cristiano Ronaldo personally.

Ronaldo felt the impact of COVID first-hand at the beginning of the 2020-21 season. He scored three goals in Juventus's first two games of the season. Ronaldo then went away to play with his Portuguese compatriots in the UEFA Nations League. Unfortunately, he contracted COVID on this trip. The dangerous virus kept Ronaldo out for three weeks.[xli] Thankfully, it did not take him nearly as long to reclaim the strong form he had shown at the start of the season. In his first game back following his illness, on November 1, 2020, the legendary striker scored two goals in just 35 minutes of action against Spezia.

Ronaldo scoring goals was about the only positive for Juventus in the 2020-21 season as COVID-19 continued to have a huge impact. In addition to players like Ronaldo catching COVID, team finances were absolutely obliterated by the pandemic. Safety restrictions prevented fans from attending matches, thus that vital income was lost, and COVID had a negative impact on financial markets outside of the world of soccer as well. Very few clubs were hit harder than Juventus.

Reports claim the Italian giant lost over $250 million during the first two years of the pandemic.[xlii] The club was forced to slash salaries, lay off workers, and cut costs wherever possible.[xliii]

Well, that is at least what the club *said* they were doing. But in reality, the club was secretly funneling money to players in order to pass Serie A and Champions League financial regulations.[xliv] Players were forced to accept this deal, which led to a very unhealthy atmosphere at the club.[xlv] One of the most-impacted players put into this tricky situation was Ronaldo. Juventus wrote off at least $20 million of his nearly $60 million salary and promised to repay him by other means.[xlv]

Despite all this controversy, Ronaldo put up another legendary season. The striker finished the season with 36 goals in 44 matches. Furthermore, 29 of these goals came in the league. No player scored more league goals than his 29, so Ronaldo was awarded Italy's Capocannoniere, an award which is traditionally given to the top Serie A goal scorer.

This was the fifth time in Ronaldo's career that he finished a season as the top scorer in a league. He also won the 2021 Coppa Italia with his Juventus teammates. Unfortunately, this was the only major trophy they won in the 2020-21 season. Inter Milan dethroned Juventus as Serie A champions, stopping the club from winning its 10th straight Serie A title. The Old Lady also had another disappointing Champions League campaign that ended in the Round of 16.

After three lackluster seasons at Juventus, Ronaldo and the club were willing to part ways. He played just 30 minutes of the first game of Juventus's 2021-22 campaign before it was announced that Ronaldo would be allowed to leave. Because the superstar's exit was imminent, Ronaldo was no longer training with Juventus or playing in matches for the club. This allowed him to focus on finding a new home, which was something that proved to be very difficult for the aging star.

Chapter 6: Return to Manchester United

2021 Offseason: A Transfer Saga brings Ronaldo Back to Old Trafford

Manchester United was the club with which Ronaldo had established himself as the best player in the world, so it makes sense that he would end up back at the same club near the end of his career. However, his return to the club was not easy.

In addition to the fact that Juventus wanted a transfer fee for Ronaldo, there were issues with his salary. Ronaldo wanted to leave Italy because of unpaid wages, so he was not going to make the same mistake again by joining a club that could not pay him what he was worth.

In August 2021, Ronaldo was 36 years old, but despite his advancing age, he was still one of the best players in the world, and someone who could contribute significantly to a big European team. And he wanted to be paid like one.

Unfortunately, there were very few clubs that could afford a player like him at the time. The world was still in the middle of the COVID-19 pandemic. Many countries were still dealing with limited crowds, stalled economies, and numerous other ramifications of the pandemic. Frankly, even under normal circumstances, only a handful of teams in the world could afford a superstar like Ronaldo.

In 2021, the big Spanish clubs who could normally afford Ronaldo, like Real Madrid, Atletico Madrid, and Barcelona, could not sign him because of new La Liga financial rules.[xlv] In Italy, Juventus was the only club with the financial might to afford a player like Ronaldo. They obviously were not in a position to keep him in 2021. France's Paris Saint-Germain could have signed him, but they had their sights on Lionel Messi instead following his shock exit from Barcelona.[xlvi]

Meanwhile, German clubs are not known for signing older superstars who are in the twilight of their careers and they are especially against paying huge fees and salaries to aging players. So, the big German clubs like Bayern Munich and Borussia Dortmund were not options for Ronaldo either.

Thus, with no Spanish, Italian, German, or French teams able or willing to sign Ronaldo, this just left English Premier League teams.

The "Big 6" of Manchester United, Liverpool, Arsenal, Chelsea, Tottenham Hotspur, and Manchester City could all have afforded Ronaldo at the time. However, only Man City were willing to actually make an offer.[xlvii]

Man City, Ronaldo, and Juventus agreed to a deal in late August. But this all changed once Ronaldo got calls and text messages from his old manager and Manchester United teammates indicating that they were not keen on his choice. Former players like United legends Rio Ferdinand and Wayne Rooney, along with their former manager Sir Alex Ferguson, reached out to Ronaldo telling him that it would be a mistake and could hurt his legacy if he were to join Manchester United's rivals, Man City.[xlviii]

These arguments would prove to be very convincing. Ronaldo ultimately turned down Man City and officially rejoined Manchester United on August 27th, 2021.[xlix]

2021-2023: Disappointing Return and Clashes with Erik ten Hag

Returning to a former club is always risky. If it goes well, a player will cement their status as a legend and forever be remembered fondly at the club. If it goes poorly, a player's legacy can be tainted forever. Instead of being remembered fondly for their first stint, they could end up being remembered for their poor second era at the club.

This is why some players have a "never look back" mentality and refuse to play for their old clubs. Unfortunately for Ronaldo, he probably should have had this mentality as well. Ronaldo's second stint at Manchester United lasted less than a season and a half.

It started strong, though. He scored goals in his second debut for Manchester United in a 4-1 win against Newcastle United. In fact, Ronaldo scored a lot of goals. In the 2021-22 season, he tallied 24 goals, more than any other player at the club.

However, Manchester United did not win a single trophy, and fired their manager just two months into the season. The club finished the season in 6th place, their first finish outside the top four in two seasons. It was also the first time Ronaldo finished a club season without a trophy since the 2010 season, his first at Real Madrid when he was sidelined with injuries.

The 2021-2022 Manchester United season was so bad for Ronaldo that he tried to leave the club that summer. He was concretely linked to Chelsea, PSG, and teams in Saudi Arabia. However, he ultimately decided to stay. This would prove to be another mistake for Ronaldo.

Manchester United had hired Ajax manager Erik ten Hag to be their new coach ahead of the 2022-2023 season. The new Dutch manager and Ronaldo clashed instantly. It was oil and water from the start.

Ronaldo was benched by ten Hag in the preseason. In a later interview, Ronaldo claimed that he was disrespected by the club, ten Hag, and everyone else at Manchester United.[l] He particularly criticized the club for not allowing him to grieve and spend time with his family following the stillbirth of one of his twins during the 2022 season.[li]

All this drama culminated with Manchester United and Ronaldo mutually agreeing to terminate his contract with the club on November 22, 2022.[li]

Chapter 7: Al Nassr

Ronaldo officially put the nightmare of his second time at Manchester United behind him on December 30, 2022, when agreed to join Saudi Arabian club Al Nassr.[lii] The three-year contract deal was officially confirmed on January 1, 2023.[liii] Reports claim that Ronaldo's new salary was just over $200 million per season.[liv]

At the time, this transfer was utterly shocking.[lv] American, Chinese, Qatari, and even Japanese clubs had spent big on legendary players approaching the end of their careers, but this was relatively new territory for Saudi Arabian clubs.

Before Ronaldo came to the country, the Saudi Pro League's biggest player was arguably Nigerian Odion Ighalo, who happened to also be a former Manchester United player.

With all due respect to Ighalo, he is not Ronaldo. The suspect quality of the Saudi League was made very clear at the end of Ronaldo's first season.

Ronaldo played just half of the 2022-23 Saudi Arabian season. Despite this, he was still one of the league's top five goal scorers. He finished the season with 14 league goals in just 16 matches. Because he joined the club so late, he was unable to help Al Nassr win any trophies. However, he would help them get their first trophy in August 2023 when Ronaldo and Al Nassr lifted the 2023 Arab Club Champions Cup. Ronaldo was the competition's top goal scorer.

While success and trophies on the pitch are always nice, Ronaldo's real legacy in Saudi Arabia is off the field. In January 2023, he was the first real star to ever make the huge move to Saudi Arabia. By the end of the 2023 summer, moving to Saudi Arabia was very normal. Huge stars like Neymar Jr., Karim Benzema, N'Golo Kanté, and numerous others followed in Ronaldo's footsteps by joining Saudi Arabian clubs in 2023.[v]

Attracting these players to the Saudi League was a part of the nation's new economic diversification plan, Saudi Vision 2030. In the context of soccer, these signings are intended to raise the quality of the nation's domestic league and transform Saudi soccer culture. Whether this plan will actually work is still to be seen. But if it does, the Ronaldo transfer to Al Nassr will always be remembered as the move that sparked it all.

Chapter 8: International Career

Ronaldo's amazing club career is just one aspect of his legend as one of the best players in the history of soccer. The other aspect you must consider is his international career.

In soccer, some players' legacies are completely confined to the international game. For example, Colombia's James Rodríguez will always be remembered as one of the best players in the world—for a short period of time—because of his efforts at the 2014 World Cup.

Other players, players who are better than Rodríguez, use international tournaments to cement themselves as some of the game's greatest players ever. Pelé, Maradona, and even Messi would not be considered the best ever if they did not perform with their national teams as well.

Unlike those aforementioned players, Ronaldo has not won a World Cup, but even without that trophy, his international record proves why he deserves to be considered one of the game's greatest players all the same.

2003-2006: Debut and Portugal's 2004 European Championship

The first time Ronaldo put on a Portugal shirt was when he was just a child. In 2001, when Ronaldo was barely a teenager, he represented Portugal with the Under-15 team at the 2001 European Youth Summer Olympic Festival.

Between 2001 and 2003, he would quickly move up the youth ranks, similar to how he quickly rose to join the first team at Sporting Club. After progressing through the Under-15, Under-17, Under-20, Under-21, and Under-23 teams in those two short years, Ronaldo was called up to the Portugal senior team.

On August 20, 2003, when he was just 18 years old (and only eight days after he moved to Manchester United), Ronaldo made his senior debut for Portugal. The youngster came on as a substitute for Luis Figo in a match against Kazakhstan.

It was impossible to know at the time, but that particular moment can now be seen as a passing of the torch from one legend to another, as Figo was Portugal's best player and one of the best in the world. The legend had some advice for Ronaldo before he came onto the field.

"Stay calm," Figo told Ronaldo as he was being substituted on. "Just play as if you were at your club."[lvi]

Ronaldo took this advice to heart. Within his five minutes of action for Portugal, the teenager intercepted a pass, skillfully dribbled up the field, and confidently took a shot on goal. His goal was saved and tipped out for a corner, but it was a sign of what Portuguese fans would see much more of in the future.

If there were any doubts that Ronaldo was destined to be Figo's successor, Ronaldo quieted them at the 2004 UEFA European Football Championship, which was hosted by Portugal.

Figo was 31 years old at the time, and had over 100 caps going into the 2004 Euros. Ronaldo, who had just finished his first season with Manchester United, was 19 years old and had only six Portugal appearances to his name. Despite Figo's experience, huge name, and ginormous legacy, Ronaldo was the better player at the 2004 Euros.

The 19-year-old Ronaldo scored two goals in his inaugural tournament with the Portuguese senior team. Figo scored none. Ronaldo was also named in the UEFA Team of the Tournament, alongside Figo. Unfortunately, the 2004 Euros will always be a bittersweet tournament for Ronaldo. On one hand, it was his very first major international tournament with Portugal. On the other hand, it ended in a crushing defeat.

Portugal lost 0-1 to Greece in the final of the tournament. Over 60,000 fans watched Portugal, a team full of some of the best attackers in the world, lose at home to a Greek side built on solid defense and time-wasting tactics. The loss was so severe that Figo retired from international football afterward. For Ronaldo, though, this was just the start.

Ronaldo made 11 appearances for Portugal in 2005 and helped them qualify for the 2006 World Cup. As big as the 2004 Euros were for Ronaldo, the 2006 World Cup was the most impactful competition of his young career to date. The reason for this was because it nearly cost him his club career.

2006 World Cup: Becoming Public Enemy Number One in Manchester

Ronaldo made his debut for Portugal all the way back in 2003 when he was just 18 years old. Shortly thereafter, he became a regular for Portugal. Ronaldo played nearly every game for his nation at the 2004 European Championships in Portugal, where the Portuguese national team finished runners-up to Greece. Ronaldo was named in the UEFA Team of the Tournament for that competition, but it would be just the start of his big tournament performances for Portugal. His next big showcase would be the 2006 World Cup.

Portugal came into the 2006 World Cup as one of the favorites due to their strong performances at the 2004 Euros. England, the country where Ronaldo played his club soccer, was also one of the big favorites, as they were in the midst of their "Golden Generation" with players like David Beckham, Wayne Rooney, and Frank Lampard.

Both England and Portugal qualified from the Group Stage at the top of their groups. They both would also win their Round of 16 fixtures against the Netherlands and Ecuador, respectively. These results meant that England and Portugal would play in the quarterfinals against each other, as they did in the 2004 Euros.

For Ronaldo, this match was arguably the biggest of his career. He was playing against the nation he called home and against many of his Manchester United teammates. However, Ronaldo did not treat this match, or his Man U teammates, like they were anything outside of the norm. This ultimately came back to hurt the young Ronaldo.

In the 62nd minute of the Portugal vs. England match, Ronaldo's Manchester United teammate Wayne Rooney was given a red card and expelled from the match for stomping on the groin of Portugal's Ricardo Carvalho following a tussle for the ball.

The referee did not give Rooney a card, however, until several Portuguese players got in his face and demanded he card the Englishman. Of course, the most notable of these players demanding that Rooney be sent off was Ronaldo himself. In fact, he was the first to charge the referee and demand action. Rooney took offense to this and began a shoving match with his Manchester United teammate. After Rooney got his red card, Ronaldo was caught on camera winking at Rooney.

Portugal then won the match via a penalty shootout, where Ronaldo scored the winning penalty, but would end up getting knocked out of the tournament in the next round by a legendary France side led by Zinedine Zidane.

Back in England, there were celebrations when Portugal was knocked out. Ronaldo's actions against England, and against Rooney specifically, had made him the most hated man in the country.

Things got so bad between himself and the English public that Ronaldo actually requested to be transferred away from Manchester United.

"I think I should get out of Manchester. The circumstances are not right to keep playing in Manchester. In two or three days I will decide where to go. I always said I wanted to play in Spain. Nobody stood up for me at Manchester, although I did not do anybody any harm," Ronaldo said before the start of the 2006-2007 season.[xxiv]

Thankfully for Manchester United fans, the club did not sell Ronaldo. The hubbub died down, and the wonderkid stayed in Manchester and soon established himself as one of the best players in the world.

2007-2011: 2008 Euros, Becoming Portugal's Captain, and the 2010 World Cup

The span of years from 2007 through 20011 was arguably the most whirlwind time of Ronaldo's club soccer career. The Portuguese superstar was nominated for his first Ballon d'Or in 2007. He ended up winning the award, the first of his career, just one year later in 2008. Ronaldo made his move to Real Madrid during this period too, as the Spanish giants signed him away from Manchester United in 2009.

To sum it all up, this period was when Ronaldo took a leap from being a very good player to becoming arguably the best player in the world. The same meteoric rise took place for Ronaldo with the national team during this time as well.

Following his and Portugal's disappointment at the 2004 Euros and 2006 World Cup, Ronaldo was chosen to be the leader of Portugal's next generation of amazing soccer players. Portuguese Football Federation vice-president, Carlos Silva, named Ronaldo as Portugal National team captain before a friendly against Brazil in February 2007.

Normally, it is the managers who name captains, but Silva's request was honored since he passed away just two days before the match.[lvii] However, this was just a temporary measure. Ronaldo would not be named permanent Portugal captain until after the 2008 UEFA European Football Championship.

At the 2008 Euros, Ronaldo and his Portugal side played well, but they unfortunately ran into one of the best teams in the world at the time, and that happened early in the tournament.

Portugal started the tournament strong by winning their first two Group Stage matches against Turkey and the Czech Republic, respectively. Ronaldo scored a goal in the latter of those two matches. The Portuguese team was shut out in their final group stage game and lost 2-0 to Switzerland. This proved to be a bad omen for Portugal. Ronaldo and his teammates lost 2-3 to

Germany in the quarterfinals. Ronaldo did not score in that match, meaning he scored just one goal in the entire tournament. Portugal fired its manager, Luiz Felipe Scolari, following the disappointing defeat.

Their next manager was someone very familiar to Ronaldo, and a person he liked very much. Portugal hired former Sporting Club manager and Manchester United coach Carlos Queiroz. This is the man who many claim is responsible for bringing Ronaldo to Manchester United, and who was Sir Alex Ferguson's right-hand man for most of the time Ronaldo was at United.

Queiroz was so important to Ronaldo's move to Manchester United that the transfer was actually negotiated in Queiroz's apartment in Lisbon.[lviii] Queiroz described bringing Ronaldo to Manchester United as his "duty as a friend and coach" to Sir Alex Ferguson and Manchester United. To sum it up, Queiroz was an integral figure in Ronaldo's club career. And he was now going to be the most important figure for Ronaldo at the international level.

One of the first things Queiroz did was make Ronaldo the permanent captain of the Portuguese national team. He did this in July 2008, just days after being appointed as Portugal manager.

Ronaldo would not live up to his new title immediately. The newly appointed captain did not score a single goal for Portugal during their 2010 World Cup qualifying campaign. Without Ronaldo's goals, Portugal nearly missed out on going to the 2010 World Cup. Portugal only qualified for the tournament via playoff victory against Bosnia and Herzegovina.

While qualifying for the World Cup went very rough, Ronaldo turned it on at the 2010 World Cup proper in South Africa. Portugal was drawn into a group with Brazil, the Ivory Coast, and North Korea. This was a relatively easy group, and Ronaldo rose to the occasion. He scored just one goal against these three opponents, but he was still named Man of the Match in each game, proving that he was much more than just a goal scorer.

After his strong start in the group stage, Ronaldo and Portugal were knocked out of the competition in the Round of 16 in a hotly contested match against the eventual champions, Spain.

This was the second straight major tournament in which Portugal failed to advance past the first knockout round. Pressure was starting to build on Ronaldo and Portugal. Like after the 2008 Euros, the pressure was so intense that Portugal fired their coach. The 2010 World Cup was the only major tournament Carlos Queiroz and Ronaldo would take part in together.

2011-2014: 2012 Euros Letdown, Becoming Portugal's Top Scorer, and the 2014 World Cup

Ronaldo's next chance to win an international trophy with Portugal came in 2012 at the 2012 UEFA European Football Championship in Poland and Ukraine. Ronaldo had scored seven goals in the qualifying matches for this competition, so he was coming into it much hotter than when he had failed to score even a single goal heading into the 2010 World Cup. This hot streak continued at the tournament.

Ronaldo's Portugal was drawn into a group with Germany, Denmark, and the Netherlands, which the press called at the time the "Group of Death."[lix] This is a soccer term used to describe the most difficult group at a tournament. If you are drawn into a Group of Death, good luck, because it means you have a small chance of getting out alive. Nevertheless, Ronaldo not only survived the Group of Death but he also *dominated* it. Portugal lost their first game to Germany, but after that, they easily brushed aside the Netherlands and Denmark. Ronaldo scored a goal against the Netherlands and was named Man of the Match.

After qualifying from the group stage, a quarterfinal clash with the Czech Republic was next for Portugal. Ronaldo, in the 79th minute and with the score deadlocked at 0-0, came crashing into the box. He cut across a Czech Republic defender and scored a diving header to put Portugal up 1-0. The Czechs could not equalize, so Ronaldo's goal sent Portugal to the semifinals where they would go up against their bitter rivals, Spain.

In addition to being Portugal's biggest rival, the Spaniards had knocked their Iberian neighbors out of the 2010 World Cup just two years earlier. Revenge was on the mind for Ronaldo and his Portuguese teammates. However, it ultimately was not to be. Spain was the team that came out victorious in this clash of titans.

Portugal did not make it easy for them, though. The match was scoreless through 120 minutes and culminated in a nerve-wracking penalty shootout. Ronaldo controversially opted to take the last penalty. The risk of doing this was that he might not have the chance to take a penalty if any of his earlier teammates missed their penalties.

Unfortunately, that was exactly what happened to Portugal and Ronaldo. Misses from João Moutinho and Bruno Alves, and four penalties scored by Spain, ensured that Ronaldo would not take a penalty. This was something Ronaldo was widely criticized for. Even his teammates, like Nani, called out Ronaldo's supposed diva behavior in this moment by saying that Ronaldo "demanded" to take the last penalty when he was asked not to.[lx]

The 2012 Euros slipped through Ronaldo's fingers in controversial fashion, but he did not let it linger on his mind for long. The Portuguese phenomenon again had a dominating qualifying campaign. Ronaldo scored eight goals during the 2014 World Cup qualifying cycle. In the leadup to the tournament, Ronaldo also reached a major milestone in his career while playing in a friendly against Cameroon on March 5, 2014. Ronaldo scored twice in that match and became Portugal's all-time goal scorer with 48 goals.

Once at the 2014 World Cup, Ronaldo and Portugal were again drawn into the tournament's Group of Death, which this time featured the United States, Ghana, and Portugal's old foe, Germany.

Portugal was able to survive the Group of Death at the 2012 Euros, but they could not do it again at the 2014 World Cup. Portugal's opening match of the tournament was against Germany. Previous matches between these teams were tight, cagey, and entertaining matches that typically could have gone either way. This match, however, was a nightmare for the Portuguese. Germany hammered Portugal 4-0. Ronaldo called this loss "the worst possible way" to start a World Cup.[xiv]

Against the United States in their second match, Ronaldo conjured up a moment of brilliance and delivered a pinpoint cross in the 95th minute to Silvestre Varela for Portugal's equalizing goal in the game. That match ended 2-2, which meant that Portugal still had a chance to qualify. They just needed to get a big win against Ghana in the final group stage game.

Portugal would end up getting the win, but not the one they needed. Ronaldo scored one of two goals for Portugal and saw his team overcome the Black Stars by a 2-1 margin. However, the huge defeat to Germany earlier in the tournament meant that Portugal had a worse goal difference than the U.S., so the Americans advanced out of the group with Germany at Portugal's expense.

The 2014 World Cup was nothing short of a disaster for Ronaldo and Portugal. This was the first time in his career that he had been knocked out in the group stage of an international tournament. Losing on such a big stage was a major blow to the legendary striker.

"It was bad," Ronaldo said, talking about having to return to Portugal after getting knocked out of the group stage at the 2014 World Cup.[xiv]

2015-2016: Winning the 2016 Euros

After disappointing exits in every major international tournament that he had played in so far in his career, the pressure was building on Ronaldo. He was at a crossroads. He had achieved enormous success with his clubs, but without a major tournament win, many people would never consider him one of the greatest soccer players of all time. And, frankly, Father Time was catching up with Ronaldo, too. He was 31 years old in 2016. This is about the age many players start to experience major declines or even retire.

Luis Figo, Portugal's former talisman, retired from international soccer when he was 31 years old. So, it was clear that time was running out for Ronaldo to win a major tournament and cement his legacy. The 2016 UEFA European Football Championship in France was perhaps Ronaldo's last chance to do just that. Early on in the tournament, though, it looked like Ronaldo and Portugal were going to crash and burn again.

Portugal was drawn into a group with Iceland, Austria, and Hungary. This was by far the Portuguese's easiest tournament group in nearly a decade. Despite this being the case, Portugal did not cope well with the expectations of being favorites to win the group.

An example of their inability to cope was in the first game of the tournament. Iceland, a nation of just 350,000 people, stunned Portugal and came away from a 1-1 draw. After the match, Ronaldo showed how frustrated he was with the draw, saying that Iceland "didn't try anything" and that they were lucky.[lxi] Some people found these comments arrogant and disrespectful, while others complimented Ronaldo for his winning attitude. Whatever the case, the comments came back to bite him just one match later.

Ronaldo and his Portugal team were again held to a draw in their next game, which was against Austria. To make matters worse, Ronaldo had a chance to win the game for his side. In the 78th minute, Austria's Martin Hinteregger committed a blatant foul on Ronaldo in the box. He tackled him with a move you would be more likely to see in American football or rugby than soccer and was severely punished for it.

After being fouled, Ronaldo, with the weight of his team and his country on his back, stepped up to the penalty spot. He tried to slot the ball into the bottom left corner but pulled it too far and ended up hitting the post. The match ended in a scoreless draw, and it was starting to look like Ronaldo would be knocked out in the group stage once again.

Yet another draw on the third matchday against Hungary gave Portugal just enough points to squeak through into the knockout rounds. The group stage had been very forgiving to Portugal and Ronaldo. They did not win a single match, but still advanced to the next round. They would continue to get lucky in the knockout rounds.

Portugal's first knockout round opponents were Croatia. Like Portugal, the Croatians have a strong reputation for punching above their weight. Additionally, that 2016 Croatia team was right in the middle of their golden generation. This was not going to be an easy match for Portugal. During the game, Croatia showed their quality, especially in the air. The Croatians were so dominant aerially all throughout the match. They really should have scored at least two goals from headers.

Somehow, they did not. In the 117th minute, Ronaldo and Ricardo Quaresma made the Croatians pay for not scoring earlier in the match. Ronaldo got the ball out wide and squared it back into the box for Quaresma, who headed the ball into the goal with a thrusted header just in front of the goal. The referee blew the whistle minutes later. 1-0 Portugal. They were going to the next round and would play Poland.

Like in the Croatia game, Portugal and Poland were tied at the end of regular time. Unlike in the Croatia game, Ronaldo and Portugal did not score in extra time. Penalties would decide this match.

Ronaldo learned his mistake from the 2012 Euros. Instead of waiting to take the last penalty, Ronaldo took the first one. He hammered it home, which set the tone for the rest of his Portuguese teammates. No Portugal player missed a penalty in the shootout. They were going to the semifinals. Their opponent was Wales, who proved to be their easiest of the tournament so far. Portugal quickly dispatched the Welsh 2-0 thanks to goals from Ronaldo and Nani.

Beating Wales meant Portugal was going to the finals to play France. However, Ronaldo would not be going with them. Well, at least not all the way with them. Ronaldo started the match but was forced off the field with an injury midway through the first half. A distraught-looking Ronaldo had to leave the match on a stretcher because his injury was so severe.

Even though he could no longer help his team on the pitch, Ronaldo was able to inspire them from the bench. Portugal's captain was regularly seen standing near the sideline by Portugal's manager Fernando Santos, which has caused many to joke that Ronaldo was Portugal's assistant coach in this match.

With Ronaldo's help from the sidelines, Portugal was able to finish the match 0-0. The match was scrappy and frankly a bit dull, just like the rest of Portugal's matches in the 2016 Euros. But whatever you want to call it, it was effective. Portugal's Eder scored in the 109th minute, putting Portugal up 1-0 over France.

Portugal and Ronaldo were European champions. He had finally gotten the trophy he had been chasing since he was 19 years old. Ronaldo did it and will forever be remembered for conquering Europe.

2017-2020: Scoring 100 International Goals for Portugal

As big as an achievement winning the 2016 Euros was for Ronaldo, he was not ready to give up on his international career just yet. Just two years after lifting the European Championship trophy, Ronaldo and his Portuguese teammates flew to Russia to represent their nation at the 2018 World Cup. Portugal's group at this tournament featured their regional rivals Spain and Morocco as well as Iran, who were managed by Ronaldo's old manager with Portugal, Carlos Queiroz.

Portugal's first match was one of the best in the entire tournament, largely because of Ronaldo's heroic efforts. This match was against Spain. Portugal got out early with a Ronaldo penalty goal in the fourth minute. Spain came back and equalized in the 24th minute. Ronaldo got another goal in the 44th, which put Portugal up 2-1 going into halftime. The Spaniards came out firing in the second half and scored two quick goals within the space of three minutes. Spain held on to their 3-2 lead for much of the second half, then, in the 88th minute, Ronaldo scored his third goal and tied the match. This was his first-ever hat trick at a World Cup.

Ronaldo scored again in the second match against Morocco. His lone goal was the difference-maker, and Portugal won that match 1-0. He did not get a goal against his old manager and Iran in the third match, but Portugal's win and two draws were enough to see them advance to the next round of the tournament.

Like so many tournaments before, this round would be where Portugal ended their run. Ronaldo and Portugal were knocked out in the Round of 16 by Uruguay in a 2-1 loss.

After the World Cup, Ronaldo missed several Portugal matches due to injury. When he came back, he scored a goal for Portugal against Luxembourg on November 17, 2019, to help them secure a place at the 2020 European Championships. This goal was his 99th ever for Portugal. Ronaldo was not set to play for Portugal until the next March, meaning that March 2020 was the earliest Ronaldo could score his 100th goal for Portugal. As we all know, something else happened in March 2020—the COVID-19 pandemic.

COVID stopped Ronaldo from playing for Portugal until September 2020. It also stopped the European Championships from taking place that summer. The wait was worth it for Ronaldo, though. On September 8, 2020, Ronaldo scored two goals for Portugal against Sweden. These goals put him over the 100-goal mark. Ronaldo was only the second male player to reach this milestone, and the first European player to hit it.

2020-Present: What's Next

Ronaldo was a part of Portugal's squads at the 2020 Euros, which were held in 2021, and the 2022 World Cup, but it was clear that his best was behind him for Portugal. Yes, he was still scoring goals, but it now seemed like the rest of his teammates were being hurt by Ronaldo and not being assisted by him—or at least that was what the critics were saying. Of course, if you asked Ronaldo, he would say he was still the best player on the team.[lxii]

So, who is right? It is impossible to say. However, we do know that Portugal underachieved at both the 2020 Euros and 2022 World Cup. Like in many prior tournaments, the Portuguese were eliminated early in the knockout rounds at both the 2020 and 2022 tournaments.

Portugal's new manager, Roberto Martínez, has not yet decided what to do with Ronaldo. So far, he has started and been a key player for Martinez's Portugal, but many expect that to change in the near future. Ronaldo could be more of a bench player for

Portugal. If he is unwilling to accept that, he could be done with Portugal forever.

Only time will tell how Ronaldo's international career ultimately ends. For now, the best thing we can do is just watch Ronaldo and enjoy him while we still can.

Chapter 9: Personal Life

Ronaldo's biggest rival throughout his career was Lionel Messi. On the field, the two iconic players showed similar levels of leadership, flair, and, of course, similar talents. However, off the field, we know much more about Ronaldo than Messi. Even though he is a global superstar, Ronaldo actively engaged with his fans and let them into his life more than any other soccer player ever, except for maybe David Beckham. This is blatantly obvious when it comes to Ronaldo's family.

Whether it is children, his parents, or other family members, Ronaldo has always been very open with his fans. For example, he has spoken about not drinking alcohol because of his father's own problems with it, which eventually killed him.

Besides making him a non-drinker, Ronaldo's parents had a big impact on his career. He is one of the most driven and motivated players the world of soccer has ever seen. Part of this was because of his parents.

"Proving to my family, proving to my father, that the decisions I took in the beginning at the age of 12 were the best ones," is what Ronaldo said when asked about what keeps him motivated.[xiv]

His father's death had a big motivating impact on Ronaldo's life, especially because he has kids of his own. Ronaldo lamented that he never really got to know his father because of his father's alcoholism.

"He was drunk nearly every day. When that happens, it was hard to get to know my father a bit more," Ronaldo said. "I didn't really get to know my father, from the heart. I didn't get to open up and tell him things …What frustrates me the most is the fact that he can't see all my successes as a player."[xiv]

Ronaldo's own frustration with his father not being around inspires him to be a good father to his own children now.

Ronaldo's first son, Cristiano Ronaldo Jr., was born on June 17, 2010, when Ronaldo was 25 years old. "I wanted to be a young father," said Ronaldo. "I wanted to be able to follow him during his development as a person and a man."[xiv] This is something Ronaldo's father was unable to do because of his early death from alcoholism.

Seven years after Cristiano Ronaldo Jr. was born, Ronaldo had twins with his long-term partner, Georgina Rodríguez, on November 12, 2017. The couple were again expecting twins in 2022 but tragically suffered complications during childbirth. One of the two twins did not survive. Ronaldo named the surviving child Angel, to remember the loss of her brother. This event severely affected Ronaldo and led to him taking some time off from Manchester United. The club did not approve of this, which ultimately culminated in Ronaldo leaving Manchester United in November 2022.

Besides his family, another important aspect of Ronaldo's personal life has always been that he is a health fanatic. Furthermore, Ronaldo does not have any tattoos so that he can regularly donate his blood and bone marrow.[lxiii]

Giving to charity and supporting his fans is another hallmark of what makes Ronaldo so great off the field. He has regularly donated tournament prizes to charities, such as in 2016 when he donated all €600,000 of his 2016 Euros win bonus to charity.[lxiv]

Children's hospitals and cancer research are areas in particular where Ronaldo has donated enormous sums of money. He once donated $165,000 towards a cancer research center in his native Portugal.[lxv] He also donated over a million dollars to Portuguese hospitals during the COVID-19 pandemic.[lxvi] He's also donated to numerous individual causes, including donating $83,000 to fund a child's brain surgery and donating over $350,000 to earthquake relief in Syria and Turkey in 2023.[lxvi]

All of Ronaldo's generous donations come from The Cristiano Ronaldo Foundation, which is committed to the same causes that Ronaldo has shown to care about. The foundation also runs the CR7 Museum in Madeira and promotes youth soccer all around the world.

Chapter 10: Legacy and Future

"Winning, that's the most important thing to me. It's as simple as that."[xiv]

This is one of Ronaldo's most famous quotes, and it sums up his legacy perfectly. Ronaldo was the consummate professional. He came to play every day with one thing in mind: winning. He also demanded that his teammates give the same level of effort.

"I try to fight every day, every match, throughout my career to be the best ever," is how Ronaldo described his mindset.[xiv]

When his teammates were able to bring this same energy to their careers, it worked brilliantly. Ronaldo and Real Madrid won three straight Champions Leagues because of his mindset. But, at Manchester United during his second stint with the team, he was met with players who were unwilling to give the same amount of effort. This is part of the reason it went so poorly.

Ronaldo's winning mindset also played a big role in the success of the teams he chose to play with. He left Portugal to join Manchester United, the best team in England and one of the best teams in the world. Ronaldo then left Manchester United to join Real Madrid, arguably the biggest and most successful club in the world.

Then, after winning everything there was to win with Real Madrid, he joined Juventus, the biggest club in Italy. After that, he returned home to Manchester United to make them winners once again. Finally, he moved to Saudi Arabia to play at one of the biggest clubs in Asia. Every move Ronaldo has made in his career was driven by his desire to win.

Another aspect of Ronaldo's legacy, besides winning, is that not everyone likes him.

"There are people who love me. There are people who hate me, who say that I'm arrogant, that I'm vain, or I'm this and that. That is part of my success," said Ronaldo about his haters. [lxvi]

His ability to view people who do not like him in this way is relatively rare in the world of soccer. Some players cave under the pressure of their haters and never become truly world-class players. Other players twist themselves into knots trying to please everyone.

Ronaldo did not care. He only wanted to play soccer. He knew that playing soccer his way would attract lots of haters, but he did not care. That is not to say that criticism never got to Ronaldo, however, he let it motivate him instead of bringing him down. The Ronaldo vs. Messi debate is an excellent example of this.

Who is better, Messi or Ronaldo? This question is one that must be brought up any time you talk about Ronaldo's legacy. His battles with Messi defined an entire era of football history. For over a decade, these two players were the best in the world. Messi or Ronaldo won nearly every Ballon d'Or award between 2008 and 2023. It was only in 2018 and 2022 that neither player won the award.

During this period, Messi won more Ballons d'Or awards than Ronaldo, which is another part of Ronaldo's complicated legacy. Politics, international success, and player reputation all affect who wins the award. Many Ronaldo fans still say he should have won more than Messi, and would have won more if not for the off-the-field considerations that some voters use to cast their votes.

For Ronaldo, he used Messi to motivate him.

"To see Messi win the Ballon d'Or four times in a row was difficult for me," said Ronaldo. "After he won the second or third in a row, I said, 'I'm not coming here anymore.' I have to win more Ballons d'Or."[xiv]

Ronaldo made that promise to himself after Messi had won the 2012 Ballon d'Or, his fourth straight. In 2013, Ronaldo's promise came true. He scored a remarkable 66 goals in 56 games and won the 2013 Ballon d'Or. He was not done yet, though. Ronaldo won the 2014 Ballon d'Or as well, getting over double the amount of votes that Messi got. This is also a part of Ronaldo's legacy. When he was faced with difficulties, he was never discouraged. Instead, he let the difficulty inspire him and motivate him to do better.

Now, Ronaldo's career is winding down. He is playing in Saudi Arabia and probably does not have many years left playing for Portugal. With all that being said, Ronaldo is still writing his legacy to some extent. As they say, it's never really over until it's over.

So, decades from now, we could be remembering Ronaldo as being one of the best players in the history of soccer. He could also be one of the founders of Saudi Arabian soccer, if his time at Al Nassr goes well.

Ronaldo has also spoken about founding more businesses, owning clubs, and doing more charity work. Although it is unlikely, Ronaldo's soccer story could be the least interesting thing about him when we look back decades from now.

For now, though, Ronaldo's legacy is firmly rooted in the world of soccer. He is one of Real Madrid's best players ever, the absolute best Portuguese player of all time, and one of the best players to ever play the game. His playing style has influenced an entire generation of players who still worship him today.

His legendary battles with Messi define an over-a-decade-long period in the history of soccer as well. His Champions League titles solidified the Champions League as Real Madrid's competition. And finally, his efforts with Portugal saw his home nation earn their first-ever international trophy. Even if Ronaldo's career were to end tomorrow, he will undoubtedly hold a special place in history for many generations to come.

Final Word/About the Author

Wow! You made it to the end of this book, and you're reading the About the Author section? Now that's impressive and puts you in the top 1% of readers.

Since you're curious about me, I was born and raised in Norwalk, Connecticut. Growing up, I could often be found spending many nights watching basketball, soccer, and football matches with my father in the family living room. I love sports and everything that sports can embody. I believe that sports are one of the most genuine forms of competition, heart, and determination. I write my works to learn more about influential athletes in the hopes that from my writing, you the reader can walk away inspired to put in an equal if not greater amount of hard work and perseverance to pursue your goals.

I've written these stories for over a decade, and loved every moment of it. When I look back on my life, I am most proud of not just having covered so many different athletes' inspirational stories, but for all the times I got e-mails or handwritten letters from readers on the impact my books have had on them.

So thank you from the bottom of my heart for allowing me to do work I find meaningful. I am incredibly grateful for you and your support.

If you're new to my sports biography books, welcome. I have goodies for you as a thank you from me in the pages ahead.

Before we get there though, I have a question for you…

Were you inspired at any point in this book?
If so, would you help someone else get inspired too?

You see, my mission is to inspire sports fans of all ages around the world that anything is possible through hard work and perseverance…but the only way to accomplish this mission is by reaching everyone.

So here's my ask from you:

Most people, regardless of what the saying tells them to do, judge a book by its cover (and its reviews).

If you enjoyed *Cristiano Ronaldo: The Inspiring Story of One of Soccer's Star Forwards,* please help inspire another person needing to hear this story by leaving a review.

Doing so takes less than a minute, and that dose of inspiration can change another person's life in more ways than you can even imagine.

To get that generous 'feel good' feeling and help another person, all you have to do is take 60 seconds and leave a review.

☆☆☆☆☆

If you're on Audible: hit the three dots in the top right of your device, click rate & review, then leave a few sentences about the book with a star rating.

If you're reading on Kindle or an e-reader: scroll to the bottom of the book, then swipe up and it will prompt a review for you.

If for some reason these have changed: you can head back to Amazon and leave a review right on the book's page.

Thank you for helping another person, and for your support of my writing as an independent author.

Clayton

Like what you read?
Then you'll love these too!

This book is one of hundreds of stories I've written. If you enjoyed this story on Cristiano Ronaldo, you'll love my other sports biography book series too.

You can find them by visiting my website at claytongeoffreys.com or by scanning the QR code below to follow my author page on Amazon.

Here's a little teaser about each of my sports biography book series:

Soccer Biography Books: This series covers the stories of tennis greats such as Neymar, Harry Kane, Robert Lewandowski, and more.

Basketball Biography Books: This series covers the stories of over 100 NBA greats such as Stephen Curry, LeBron James, Michael Jordan, and more.

Football Biography Books: This series covers the stories of over 50 NFL greats such as Peyton Manning, Tom Brady, and Patrick Mahomes, and more.

Baseball Biography Books: This series covers the stories of over 40 MLB greats such as Aaron Judge, Shohei Ohtani, Mike Trout, and more.

Basketball Leadership Biography Books: This series covers the stories of basketball coaching greats such as Steve Kerr, Gregg Popovich, John Wooden, and more.

Tennis Biography Books: This series covers the stories of tennis greats such as Serena Williams, Rafael Nadal, Andy Roddick, and more.

Women's Basketball Biography Books: This series covers the stories of many WNBA greats such as Diana Taurasi, Sue Bird, Sabrina Ionescu, and more.

Lastly, if you'd like to join my exclusive list where I let you know about my latest books, and gift you free copies of some of my other books, go to **claytongeoffreys.com/goodies**.

Or, if you don't like typing, scan the following QR code here to go there directly. See you there!

Clayton

References

[i] France Football. (n.d.). Palmarès Ballon d'Or: Tous Les vainqueurs année par année. *France Football.* www.francefootball.fr/ballon-d-or/palmares/
[ii] Hughes, Rob. "Ronaldo to Join Real Madrid for Record Price." *The New York Times*, The New York Times, 11 June 2009, www.nytimes.com/2009/06/12/sports/soccer/12iht-RONALDO.html
[iii] Easton, Joe, and Chiara Albanese. "Cristiano Ronaldo Transferred to Juventus by Real Madrid." *Bloomberg.Com*, Bloomberg, 10 July 2018, www.bloomberg.com/news/articles/2018-07-10/ronaldo-s-transfer-to-juventus-agreed-real-madrid-says
[iv] Luckhurst, Samuel. "Erik Ten Hag Hits Back at Cristiano Ronaldo over Manchester United Departure." *Manchester Evening News*, 9 Dec. 2022, www.manchestereveningnews.co.uk/sport/football/football-news/man-united-ten-hag-ronaldo-25715963
[v] Jabir, Wael. "Saudi Pro League Transfer Roundup: Neymar, Benzema, More." *ESPN*, ESPN Internet Ventures, 8 Sept. 2023, www.espn.com/soccer/story/_/id/37884523/saudi-pro-league-transfers-2023-deals-talks
[vi] Amir, Shady. "Ronaldo Says Saudi League Could Become Top Five in the World." *Reuters*, Thomson Reuters, 24 May 2023, www.reuters.com/sports/soccer/ronaldo-says-saudi-league-could-become-top-five-world-2023-05-24/
[vii] Jimenez, Ruben. "Cristiano Ronaldo Turns 32." *MARCA in English*, MARCA, 5 Feb. 2017, www.marca.com/en/football/real-madrid/2017/02/05/5896528d22601db9458b4599.html
[viii] Thompson, Wright. "The Father Portugal's Cristiano Ronaldo Never Really Knew." *ESPN*, ESPN Internet Ventures, 16 June 2016, www.espn.com/soccer/story/_/id/37450052/the-father-cristiano-ronaldo-never-really-knew
[ix] Plum Pictures. *Cristiano Ronaldo Meets Piers Morgan*, created by Piers Morgan, ITV, 19 Sept. 2019
[x] Eurosport UK. "Cristiano Ronaldo's Mother: I Wanted an Abortion, but God Said No." *Eurosport*, Eurosport, 5 Nov. 2015, www.eurosport.com/football/liga/2014-2015/cristiano-ronaldos-mother-i-wanted-an-abortion-but-god-said-no_sto4979169/story.shtml
[xi] "Ronaldo's Mother Reveals She Tried to Abort Her Son." *Independent.Ie*, Independent.ie, 18 July 2014, www.independent.ie/sport/soccer/other-soccer/ronaldos-mother-reveals-she-tried-to-abort-her-son/30441371.html
[xii] Lusa. "Bola de Ouro - Ronaldo Conquistou Primeiro Prémio Aos Oito

Anos No Andorinha." *Diário de Notícias*, 2 Dec. 2008, www.dn.pt/dossiers/desporto/cristiano-ronaldo/noticias/bola-de-ouro---ronaldo-conquistou-primeiro-premio-aos-oito-anos-no-andorinha-1066979.html

xiii Hayward, Ben. "The 'little Bee' Who Always Cried - the Story of Young Ronaldo's Path to Greatness in Madeira." *Goal.Com US*, Goal.com, 19 Sept. 2023, www.goal.com/en-us/news/the-little-bee-who-always-cried-the-story-of-young-ronaldos-path-/k927thno26e41b42er1z9zhqo

xiv *Ronaldo*. Directed by Anthony Wonke, On the Corner Films, We Came We Saw We Conquered Studios, Mediapro, 2015

xv Digi Sport. "Boloni Îi Aminte te de Debutul Lui Ronaldo La Sporting: 'Nu Reu eam Să Îl Opresc Să Facă Driblinguri.'" *Digi Sport*, 13 Jan. 2015, www.digisport.ro/Sport/FOTBAL/Competitii/Fotbal+International/Boloni+is i+aminteste+de+debutul+lui+Ronaldo+la+Sporting

xvi Manchester Evening News. "Clash of the Titans." *Manchester Evening News*, 13 Jan. 2013, www.manchestereveningnews.co.uk/sport/football/football-news/clash-of-the-titans-989542

xvii Eurosport UK "Liverpool Rejected Ronaldo." *Eurosport*, Eurosport, 6 Dec. 2010, www.eurosport.com/football/premier-league/2009-2010/liverpool-rejected-ronaldo_sto2572390/story.shtml

xviii Hernandez, Xavi. "FC Barcelona: 'Pude Fichar a Cristiano Por 17 Millones.'" *Marca.Com*, 1 Dec. 2016, www.marca.com/futbol/barcelona/2016/12/01/5840043d22601d243d8b4594.html

xix Clements, Ashley. "Arsene Wenger Reveals His Biggest Regret Is Missing out on Cristiano Ronaldo." *Daily Mail Online*, 18 Sept. 2014, www.dailymail.co.uk/sport/football/article-2760722/Arsene-Wenger-reveals-biggest-regret-missing-Cristiano-Ronaldo.html

xx Pilger, Sam. "'He Was There to Put on a Show': Ronaldo's Legendary Manchester United Audition." *Bleacher Report*, 14 Oct. 2017, bleacherreport.com/articles/2735948-he-was-there-to-put-on-a-show-ronaldos-legendary-manchester-united-audition

xxi Marshall, Adam. "United Confirm Ronaldo Capture." *Sky Sports*, 12 Aug. 2003, www.skysports.com/football/news/2273339/united-confirm-ronaldo-capture

xxii Dawson, Rob. "Flashback to Ronaldo's Manchester United Debut." *ESPN.Com*, ESPN, 15 Aug. 2018, www.espn.co.uk/football/story/_/id/37501077/flashback-cristiano-ronaldo-manchester-united-debut-vs-bolton.

[xxiii] Stirling, James. "Ronaldo: I Can't Stay in Manchester." *The Guardian*, Guardian News and Media, 9 July 2006, www.theguardian.com/football/2006/jul/09/worldcup2006.sport3

[xxiv] Gardner, Alan. "Football: FIFA Will Take No Action over Real Madrid's Pursuit of Cristiano Ronaldo." *The Guardian*, Guardian News and Media, 16 June 2008, www.theguardian.com/football/2008/jun/16/ronaldo.manchesterunited

[xxv] Taylor, Daniel. "I Am a Slave, Says Ronaldo as He Pushes for Madrid Move." *The Guardian*, Guardian News and Media, 10 July 2008, www.theguardian.com/football/2008/jul/11/manchesterunited.premierleague1

[xxvi] "*Ronaldo* Ankle Surgery a 'Success.'" BBC News, BBC, 7 July 2008, news.bbc.co.uk/sport2/hi/football/teams/m/man_utd/7486670.stm

[xxvii] "Cristiano Ronaldo Welcomed by 80,000 Fans at Real Madrid Unveiling." *The Guardian*, Guardian News and Media, 6 July 2009, www.theguardian.com/football/2009/jul/06/cristiano-ronaldo-real-madrid-bernabeu

[xxviii] Glendenning, Barry. "Champions League: Milan v Real Madrid - as It Happened." *The Guardian*, Guardian News and Media, 3 Nov. 2009, www.theguardian.com/football/2009/nov/03/milan-real-madrid-latest-score

[xxix] Walker, Ron. "The Day Jose Mourinho's 'special One' Tag Was Born: When the Enigma Announced Himself to the Premier League." *Sky Sports*, Sky Sports, 20 Mar. 2023, www.skysports.com/football/story-telling/12040/12838761/the-day-jose-mourinhos-special-one-tag-was-born-when-the-enigma-announced-himself-to-the-premier-league

[xxx] Feehely, Alan. "Carlo Ancelotti Explains the Secret to His Famed Man-Management Ability." *Football España*, Football Espana, 11 May 2022, www.football-espana.net/2022/05/11/carlo-ancelotti-explains-the-secret-to-his-famed-man-management-ability

[xxxi] ESPN.com. "Real Madrid Star Cristiano Ronaldo: 'You Have to Be Ambitious.'" *ESPN*, ESPN Internet Ventures, 15 Jan. 2015, www.espn.com/soccer/story/_/id/37398372/real-madrid-star-cristiano-ronaldo-says-be-ambitious

[xxxii] "Un Histórico Ronaldo Lidera La Goleada Al Espanyol." *LALIGA*, LALIGA, 12 Sept. 2015, www.laliga.es/noticias/un-historico-ronaldo-lidera-la-goleada-al-espanyol

[xxxiii] ESPN Staff. "Cristiano Ronaldo Scores 500th Career Goal." *ESPN.Com*, ESPN, 30 Sept. 2015, www.espn.co.uk/football/story/_/id/37434631/real-madrid-cristiano-ronaldo-scores-500th-career-goal

[xxxiv] Estepa, Javier. "Zinedine Zidane Takes Twitter by Storm." *MARCA*

English, MARCA, 5 Jan. 2016, www.marca.com/en/football/real-madrid/2016/01/05/568c3c1be2704e72648b4639.html.

[xxxv] Corrigan, Dermot. "Ronaldo: 'It's Been Very Nice Playing for Real.'" *ESPN*, ESPN, 26 May 2018, www.espn.co.uk/football/real-madrid/story/3510863/cristiano-ronaldo-puts-future-in-doubt-its-been-very-nice-playing-for-real-madrid

[xxxvi] Winterburn, Chris. "Real Madrid: Everything You Need to Know about Cristiano Ronaldo's Real Future." *MARCA in English*, MARCA, 27 May 2018, www.marca.com/en/football/real-madrid/2018/05/27/5b0aa06be2704eb84f8b459c.html

[xxxvii] "Cristiano Ronaldo Signs for Juventus!" *Juventus.Com*, Juventus, 10 June 2020, www.juventus.com/en/news/articles/cristiano-ronaldo-signs-for-juventus

[xxxviii] BBC Sport. "Cristiano Ronaldo: Juventus Sign Real Madrid Forward for £99.2m." *BBC Sport*, BBC, 10 July 2018, www.bbc.com/sport/football/44785173

[xxxix] BBC Sport. "Coronavirus: All Sport in Italy Suspended Because of Outbreak." *BBC Sport*, BBC, 9 Mar. 2020, www.bbc.com/sport/51808683

[xl] Fiore, Tommaso. "Serie A to Resume on June 20 Once Coppa Italia Marks Season Restart." *Sky Sports*, Sky Sports, 29 May 2020, www.skysports.com/football/news/11854/11996335/serie-a-to-resume-on-june-20-following-italian-government-approval

[xli] McIntyre, Doug. "Cristiano Ronaldo Returns from Covid-19, Scores Twice in Juventus Win." *Yahoo! Sports*, Yahoo!, 1 Nov. 2020, sports.yahoo.com/cristiano-ronaldo-returns-from-covid-19-scores-twice-juventus-win-video-164145440.html

[xlii] Associated Press. "Juventus Reports $250m in Losses amid Covid-19 Pandemic." *Sportsnet.Ca*, 17 Sept. 2021, www.sportsnet.ca/soccer/article/juventus-reports-250m-losses-amid-covid-19-pandemic/

[xliii] Reuters. "Juventus Players Waive Four Months' Wages Due to Coronavirus Outbreak." *The Guardian*, Guardian News and Media, 28 Mar. 2020, www.theguardian.com/football/2020/mar/28/juventus-players-wages-coronavirus-serie-a

[xliv] Jones, Tobias. "'I Feel like I'm Selling My Soul': Inside the Crisis at Juventus." *The Guardian*, Guardian News and Media, 25 Apr. 2023, www.theguardian.com/football/2023/apr/25/inside-the-crisis-at-juventus-andrea-agnelli-fabio-paratici-plusvalenze

[xlv] Ivanov, Kalin. "A New Dawn for FFP and the Expected Impact of the New Rules." *Linklaters*, 7 Oct. 2021, www.linklaters.com/en-

us/insights/blogs/sportinglinks/2021/october/a-new-dawn-for-ffp-and-the-expected-impact-of-the-new-rules

[xlvi] BBC Sport. "Lionel Messi Signs Two-Year Paris St-Germain Deal after Leaving Barcelona." *BBC Sport*, BBC, 10 Aug. 2021, www.bbc.co.uk/sport/football/58163106

[xlvii] Delaney, Miguel. "Man City Agree Personal Terms with Cristiano Ronaldo." *The Independent*, Independent Digital News and Media, 26 Aug. 2021, www.independent.co.uk/sport/football/cristiano-ronaldo-man-city-news-b1909193.html

[xlviii] Ogden, Mark. "Cristiano Ronaldo's Man Utd Return: Ex-Teammates' Whatsapp Messages Helped End Man City Move - Sources." *ESPN*, ESPN Internet Ventures, 27 Aug. 2021, www.espn.com/soccer/story/_/id/37620172/ex-teammates-whatsapp-messages-helped-end-man-city-move-sources

[xlix] Aarons, Ed, and Fabrizio Romano. "'Welcome Back': Manchester United Agree €20m Deal for Cristiano Ronaldo." *The Guardian*, Guardian News and Media, 27 Aug. 2021, www.theguardian.com/football/2021/aug/27/manchester-city-cristiano-ronaldo-wants-to-leave-juventus-allegri

[l] Wake Up TV Productions. *Cristiano Ronaldo World Exclusive*, created by Piers Morgan, TalkTV, 16 Nov. 2022.

[li] Dawson, Rob. "Cristiano Ronaldo Leaves Man United by 'Mutual Agreement.'" *ESPN*, ESPN Internet Ventures, 22 Nov. 2022, www.espn.com/soccer/story/_/id/37634146/cristiano-ronaldo-leaves-man-united-mutual-agreement

[lii] ESPN. "Cristiano Ronaldo Signs with Saudi Club Al-Nassr after Man Utd Exit." *ESPN*, ESPN Internet Ventures, 30 Dec. 2022, www.espn.com/soccer/story/_/id/37635006/cristiano-ronaldo-signs-saudi-club-al-nassr-man-utd-exit

[liii] Romano, Fabrizio. "Cristiano Ronaldo Completes Deal to Join Saudi Arabian Club Al Nassr." *The Guardian*, Guardian News and Media, 30 Dec. 2022, www.theguardian.com/football/2022/dec/30/cristiano-ronaldo-al-nassr-saudi-arabia

[liv] "Fabrizio Romano Reveals One Other Club That Bid for CR7." *Planet Football*, Planet Football, 31 Dec. 2022, www.planetfootball.com/videos/cristiano-ronaldo-transfer-al-nassr-fabrizio-romano-mls-man-utd

[lv] Wright, Chris. "Cristiano Ronaldo's Move to Saudi Arabia's Al-Nassr Joins List of Surprise Transfers out of Europe." *ESPN*, ESPN Internet Ventures, 30 Dec. 2022,

www.espn.com/soccer/story/_/id/37634818/cristiano-ronaldos-move-saudi-arabias-al-nassr-joins-list-surprise-transfers-europe

lvi Flanagan, Chris. "Long Read: Cristiano Ronaldo's Incredible Journey to 100 Portugal Goals – and the All-Time International Record He Broke This Year." *Fourfourtwo.Com*, FourFourTwo, 30 Aug. 2021, www.fourfourtwo.com/features/cristiano-ronaldo-portugal-100th-goal-international-record-man-utd-real-madrid-juventus-sweden-ali-daei

lvii "Scolari Delighted with Portugal Win over Brazil." *Rediff India*, 7 Feb. 2007, www.rediff.com/sports/2007/feb/07scol.htm

lviii Honigstein, Raphael. "Ronaldo Faces Friend-Turned-Foe When He Takes on 'dad' Carlos Queiroz and Iran in World Cup." *ESPN*, ESPN Internet Ventures, 24 June 2018, www.espn.com/soccer/story/_/id/37498639/ronaldo-friend-turned-foe-faces-dad-carlos-queiroz-iran-world-cup

lix Bevan, Chris. "Euro 2012: Who Will Survive the Group of Death?" *BBC Sport*, BBC, 16 June 2012, www.bbc.co.uk/sport/0/football/18463292

lx Foxsports. "Portugal Winger Nani Suggests That Ronaldo Demanded the Fifth Penalty against Spain to Take the Glory." *Fox Sports*, FOX SPORTS Australia, 29 June 2012, www.foxsports.com.au/football/euro-2012/portugal-winger-nani-suggests-that-ronaldo-demanded-the-fifth-penalty-against-spain-to-take-the-glory/news-story/d8b479fd8297f96af4e9a59d4a55303c

lxi Delaney, Miguel. "Cristiano Ronaldo's Iceland Criticism Was Arrogant and Did Him a Disservice." *ESPN*, ESPN Internet Ventures, 15 June 2016, www.espn.com/soccer/story/_/id/37450195/cristiano-ronaldo-iceland-criticism-was-arrogant-did-disservice

lxii Wilson, Jeremy. "Cristiano Ronaldo Slapped down by Portugal Coach for Unacceptable Reaction." *The Telegraph*, Telegraph Media Group, 9 Dec. 2022, www.telegraph.co.uk/world-cup/2022/12/05/cristiano-ronaldo-slapped-portugal-coach-unacceptable-reaction/

lxiii Goal. "Does Cristiano Ronaldo Have Tattoos? Juventus Star's Position on Body Ink Explained." *Goal.Com*, 19 Sept. 2023, www.goal.com/en/news/cristiano-ronaldo-tattoos/axdtx8bwqem01dr97j7ha755u

lxiv Critchley, Mark. "Cristiano Ronaldo: Real Madrid Forward Donates €600,000 Champions League Win Bonus to Charity." *The Independent*, Independent Digital News and Media, 3 June 2016, www.independent.co.uk/sport/football/european/cristiano-ronaldo-real-madrid-forward-donates-eu600-000-champions-league-final-bonus-to-charity-a7063036.html

[lxv] "Ronaldo's $350K Donation to Earthquake Victims in Syria and Turkey." *MARCA in English*, MARCA, 5 Mar. 2023, www.marca.com/en/football/2023/03/05/6404bb5d46163fa07c8b4599.html

[lxvi] Diaz, Natalie. "'Seven' - an ode to Cristiano Ronaldo, Real Madrid's global superstar." ESPN, ESPN Internet Ventures, 20 Mar 2018, www.espn.com/soccer/story/_/id/37493284/seven-ode-cristiano-ronaldo-espn-magazine-dominant-20

Made in United States
Troutdale, OR
10/02/2024